Praise for *Times Square Red, Times Square Blue*

"Measured but emotional, illuminating but challenging yet ultimately hopeful, *Times Square Red, Times Square Blue* is Delany's critical response to the 30-year enactment of the 'menace' of which he first read in the news . . . the fact is, [Delany] has much of interest to say about sexuality, gay and otherwise, and about the socially constructed institutions within which sexual freedom has meaning."
—*San Francisco Chronicle*

"Delany sees a continuing class war raging silently in our society. He deprecates 'networking' in favor of 'contact,' the freewheeling encounters with strangers that most New Yorkers have in public places. The new Times Square, he feels, is a symbol of the desire to stamp out contact in the name of a vaguely sinister 'safety.'"
—*New York Times Book Review*

"Samuel R. Delany never ceases to surprise his readers, mainly because he writes astonishingly well about almost anything . . . [*Times Square Red, Times Square Blue*] is both a celebration of the kaleidoscopic possibilities inherent in urban diversity and a eulogy for the plurality of human contact and stimulation squelched by the Times Square makeover."
—*Village Voice*

"In *Times Square Red, Times Square Blue*, Delany describes the subculture of the Times Square movie theatres in [the 1970s and '80s]. In the movie houses sex was not furtive; it was enjoyed openly and without fear, and yet it could only exist in this way within these marginal limits. And it involved a shared language: the men in these theatres talked about what they were doing, whom they did it with, how it went. They created a way of speaking that was as real as any other, no matter how shadowy or illicit people on the outside imagined it to be."
—*New Yorker*

Times Square Red, Times Square Blue

SEXUAL CULTURES

General Editors: Ann Pellegrini, Tavia Nyong'o, and Joshua Chambers-Letson

Founding Editors: José Esteban Muñoz and Ann Pellegrini

For a complete list of books in the series, see www.nyupress.org

Times Square Red, Times Square Blue

20th Anniversary Edition

SAMUEL R. DELANY

With a new Foreword by Robert F. Reid-Pharr

NEW YORK UNIVERSITY PRESS

New York

NEW YORK UNIVERSITY PRESS
New York

First published in paperback in 2001.

Library of Congress Cataloging-in-Publication Data
Names: Delany, Samuel R., author.
Title: Times Square red, Times Square blue / Samuel R. Delany; with a new foreword by Robert F. Reid-Pharr.
Description: 20th anniversary edition. | New York: New York Universit Press, [2019] | Series: Sexual cultures: new directions from the Center for Lesbian and Gay Studies | Includes bibliographical references and index.
Identifiers: LCCN 2018045003| ISBN 978-1-4798-8736-1 (cl: alk. paper) | ISBN 978-1-4798-2777-0 (pb: alk. paper)
Subjects: LCSH: Sex-oriented businesses—New York (State)—New York. | Sex customs—New York (State)—New York. | Times Square (New York, N.Y.)—Social life and customs. | Times Square (New York, N.Y.)—Social conditions. | Male homosexuality—New York (State)—New York. | Urban renewal—New York (State)—New York—History—20th century.
Classification: LCC HQ146.N7 D45 2019 | DDC 338.4/7306709747—dc23
LC record available at https://lccn.loc.gov/2018045003

New York University Press books are printed on acid-free paper, and their binding materials are chosen for strength and durability.

Manufactured in the United States of America
10 9 8 7 6 5 4 3

For
Bruce Benderson

Contents

Foreword

Robert F. Reid-Pharr

August 2018

For decades the governing cry of our cities has been "Never speak to strangers." I propose that in a democratic city it is imperative that we speak to strangers, live next to them, and learn how to relate to them on many levels, from the political to the sexual. City venues must be designed to allow these multiple interactions to occur easily, with a minimum of danger, comfortably, and conveniently. This is what politics—the way of living in the polis, in the city—is about.

—Samuel R. Delany, *Times Square Red, Times Square Blue*, 193

There is a vexing conceptual difficulty that one must face when considering how we might best structure our ever more complex societies, how we might manage the unruly bodies of even more unruly citizens. The question is not only one of municipal administrations or shared resources and responsibilities, but also of how we might encourage (political, social, financial, ethical, and indeed erotic) investment in our various and varied communities such that we might come to recognize our neighbors, both near and far, as neither competitors nor impediments to our efforts at survival, but instead as companions, lovers, and kin whose success and pleasure redound upon us, whose good will and fellow feeling reach us with enough force and regularity to encourage us to protect, embrace, and amplify both the most exalted dreams and the most grubby desires of even—and especially—those whose voices ring awkwardly on the ear and whose visages sit strangely on the eye.

Part of what makes Samuel R. Delany's pathbreaking work *Times Square Red, Times Square Blue* so enormously delicious, so hugely exciting to read, is the fact that Delany so ardently and unhesitatingly announces New York as a *living* city. In the tradition of the grand theorist of urban life, Jane Jacobs, whose 1961 masterpiece, *The Death and Life of Great American Cities,* Delany amplifies and redirects, *Times Square Red, Times Square Blue* focuses largely on the matter of contact, the myriad unscripted and often unsanctioned ways in which citizens interact not so much apart from capitalist forms of competition as alongside them. For Delany the real issue within the modern metropolis is how to encourage contact across differences of race, gender, religion, ethnicity, and especially class. It is this contact that provokes and underwrites the security, possibility, contentment, and astonishment that are the necessary ingredients of successful urban life. "In a democratic society that values social movement, social opportunity, and class flexibility, interclass contact is the most rewarding, productive, and thus privileged kind of contact," Delany writes. "There is no way people can move comfortably between classes if the classes themselves do not have repeated pleasant social interactions with one another, class war or not" (*Times Square Red, Times Square Blue,* 73).

Here is where Delany mounts his most trenchant theoretical intervention. That is to say, he is especially careful to note that not all forms of human interaction can be read as "contact" in the way that he frames the term. In particular, Delany situates the concept of contact against the idea of "networking," suggesting that the network opportunity—the conference, the fraternity, the professional gathering— is always established *within* the protocols of capitalist competition such that even the most convivial sites of professional and class affiliation, the office cocktail party to take one example, can offer only those opportunities and rewards that work to reinforce the limits of individual networks while reinvigorating the policing of class boundaries. In a series of hilarious send-ups of writers' conventions he notes that aspiring authors arrive at these events hoping that they will experience the type of surprising, if not exactly unanticipated, pleasures and rewards that one haphazardly encounters in interactions with (relative) strangers in the streets of New York. What these eager conferees inevitably experience, however, is the reiteration of their own class positions. Or as Delany succinctly frames the matter, "Networking produces more opportunities to network—and that's about it" (139).

While Delany is especially careful to avoid a rigorous, or perhaps better put, brittle distinction between "contact" and "network," he does suggest that the redevelopment of the area around Times Square and the destruction of many smaller establishments, including pornography theaters, in favor of skyscrapers, chain stores, and malls, is designed first and foremost to allay the fears of tourists who suspect that without the proper policing and surveillance they might trip into exactly the cross-class contact that Delany celebrates. Thus like the eager young writer who mistakes the scripted sociality of the conference for the complexities of casual social interaction, the individual who enters the New Times Square walks into an area in which the necessary acts of class exclusion have taken place already. Even with its much heralded grime and grit, Times Square existed for decades as a location dominated by working class and poor New Yorkers who were often met by middle and upper class persons specifically interested in having contact, including sexual contact, across boundaries of class and race. Today Times Square has become, or at least is imagined to have become, a location in which the middle and upper classes come to see in the streets, the shops, the malls, and the theaters exhausted versions of themselves.

I think it is fair to say that where *Times Square Red, Times Square Blue* not only rings, but also reminds the reader of how very limited a palette is most often utilized in the production of what we imagine as properly established theory or criticism, is in Delany's detailed, evocative, poignant, sometimes shocking, sometimes sad, and often naughty descriptions of the porn theaters that he frequented over a thirty year period.

> "But what," asked a young woman editor, a reader of an early draft, "went on *in* those movie theaters, before they were closed? Let me see some of that." (xxiii)

The trick for readers about to experience *Times Square Red, Times Square Blue* for the first or the forty-first time is *not* to become so focused on the many descriptions of sexual contact that Delany offers that they miss the stabbing critique embedded within those descriptions. Delany's genius turns on the fact that he is not afraid to both look and see. He sees homeless men, hustlers, crack addicts, movie attendants, sewer workers, shoe shine men, food cart operators. He sees young and old men, fat and skinny men, mentally and physically disabled men. He sees gay and straight men. He sees poor, working class, professional, and occasionally rich men. The critique that he so boldly offers to the rest of us, however, is not simply that he sees more broadly than we do, but instead that this process is surprisingly simple. What is complicated is the process of *not* seeing. Much of his critique of the *intra*-class networking that produces so much of the very literary/critical establishment of which he is himself a part is that it so rigorously enforces a sort of class-based conceptual blindness. It is very often—perhaps most often—the case that while the intellectual class may note working class and poor persons, they very infrequently hail them. They look but they do not see. Thus for Delany, the goal is not simply to titillate his readers but also to establish examples, instruments one might say, by and with which we can begin to refuse the clumsy binary between the vernacular and the expert.

In a remarkable exchange between Delany and Hoke—a bear of a man with large "Negro-wide" nostrils, a short uncut cock, a surgically corrected harelip covered by a walrus moustache, and, most appetizingly for Delany, a set of large, work-hardened, and radically nail-bitten hands—Hoke explains why after months of successful casual encounters they fail so miserably when he finally invites Delany to his apartment for a bout of fun/friendly sex.

> The reason we couldn't make it is that I don't even *wanna* like the things about me that you think are just great! I mean, I probably don't need anybody who *hates* 'em. But for any kind of regular thing, I need a guy who just

sort of ignores them, like I do—but wants to put that little girl through all her changes. I mean—what? You're thirty-six. I'm thirty-eight. What it is, see, is we're both homosexual. You need somebody the same sex as you. I need somebody the same sex as me. But that's just not each other. (102)

That is to say, Hoke offers an un-satiated Delany a succinct, complex, and deftly rendered explication of the mechanics of desire (I need you to want that aspect of my being—that little girl—obscured by my physicality) as well as the complicated instrumentality of identity (your homosexuality is not *my* homosexuality) in the few polite moments given over to his failed paramour prior to offering him the door. And lest one imagine that Delany, or I for that matter, wish to suggest that the theoretical statements of working class men are somehow more pure or sophisticated simply because they emanate from working class men, I would restate my argument that Hoke's bravura performance only repeats the idea that our networks often operate not so much by suppressing the artistic/intellectual possibilities inherent in the intricacies of cross-class contact as by ignoring them.

I will note in this regard that flouting normative standards about where and with whom sexual activity might take place has been a key method across the whole of Delany's rambling oeuvre. From the publication of his first novel, *The Jewels of Aptor*, in 1962, Delany has been playing across not only boundaries of race, class, gender, and sexuality, but also, and even more importantly, over what presumably can be imagined and said within both fiction and cultural criticism. A full or even adequate treatment of how the theme of race mixing, class mixing, gender bending, and boundary breaking function within Delany's body of work would be impossible here. Still, one sees these ideas articulated repeatedly and ever more skillfully across the decades of Delany's writing career. In his most popular novel, *Dhalgren* (1975), his underappreciated *Stars in My Pocket Like Grains of Sand* (1984), the ground-breaking four-volume series Return to Nevèrÿon, published between 1979 and 1994, his 1988 book-length autobiographical essay, *The Motion of Light in Water: Sex and Science Fic-*

tion in the East Village, his 1994 novel of philosophy, murder, and out of bounds sexual desire, *The Mad Man,* his two late novels, *Dark Reflections* (2007) and *Through the Valley of the Nest of Spiders* (2012), and of course *Times Square Red, Times Square Blue* (1999) itself, we see Delany struggling not only to break the unnecessary boundaries between man and woman, black and white, gay and straight, the vernacular and the expert, but also to encourage—and to teach—others to do the same.

In reading the two long essays that compose *Times Square Red, Times Square Blue,* many have expressed concern over the idea that by situating his critiques of the redevelopment of Times Square within porn theaters Delany effectively disappears women from his analyses of the promises and intricacies of contact. The point is made even more starkly palpable by the fact that Delany himself returns to this idea throughout the work. Speaking of a scene that exemplifies the fraternity sometimes established between men in the theaters, fraternity often generously shared across lines of race, class, *and* sexuality, Delany writes that such a scene's

> charm, sociality, and warmth—if it has any—depend entirely on the absence of "the woman"—or at least depend on flattening "the woman" till she is only an image on a screen, whether of light or memory, reduced to "pure" "sexuality," till, a magical essence, a mystical energy, she pervades, grounds, even fuels the entire process, from which she is corporally, intellectually, emotionally, and politically absent. (25)

This observation opens onto a story that Delany tells of taking his friend Ana, a stocky, dark-haired Hispanic woman who works as a daytime temp and a nighttime musician, into a theater with him. The reactions of the men whom she encounters range from unfazed to mildly shocked and pleasantly amused, until she is approached for sex.

> He asked me would I let him . . . eat me. Only, I could tell: He *really* thought I might say yes. And, when I said, "No, thank you," he smiled, shrugged—he did look sad—and . . . walked away. (29; Delany's ellipses)

This leads to Delany's repeated claim that, in fact, the forms of sociality that took place between both heterosexual and homosexual men in the Times Square porn theaters should be taken as useful models for interaction between the genders. Delany celebrates what he calls the "the unmitigated violence to the West's traditional concept of 'women'" embedded in a sentence like "He asked me would I let him . . . eat me," and perhaps even more provocatively in the rejoinder, "He *really* thought that I might say yes," precisely because these phrases refuse the idea of a cloistered female sexuality, closeted within restricted (networked) fields of operation in which the point is precisely to harass, control, and encumber women and girls. Delany has particular disdain for the idea that the supposed "cleaning up" of Times Square would create a safer space for women, arguing instead that as the destruction of buildings, businesses, and communities that preceded the renovation devastated the working class communities that inhabited and utilized the area, setting off epidemics of homelessness, drug addiction, and under-aged prostitution in the process, that at best the promised safety for women was only ever imagined to cover a minority of middle and upper class women at the expense of "out of network" women and men. At the same time, Delany ends *Times Square Red, Times Square Blue* not with an encomium to the lost joys of all male sexual contact but instead with the frank suggestion that the types of sex spaces pioneered by gay men should, in fact, be radically extended to all portions of our communities, that we should "move such institutions from the barely known and secret, from the discourse of the illicit, into the widely known, well-publicized, and generally advertised rhetoric of bourgeois elegance and convenience" (197).

I will end these comments and make way for the thrill of the fantastic essays included in this remarkable work by giving voice to the nagging fretfulness that my rereading of *Times Square Red, Times Square Blue* has engendered. I have the uncanny sense of having been here before, *déjà vécu*, of watching with glum bewilderment as a gentrification process largely centered on Manhattan twenty years ago has broken with incredible vigor onto the shores of Brooklyn, Queens, the Bronx, and even humble Staten Island. The arguments that one habitually hears about the displacement of working class and poor communities seem tepid and rehearsed as we witness the erection of a seemingly endless stream of under-populated glass and steel luxury condominiums. This has been met by a vigorous politics of gay respectability in which casual sexual encounters between men still take place, but within contexts that are corralled by rigid boundaries of race and class. Want quick sex? Apps, vacations to gay enclaves, and circuit parties all work. But in each instance there is a quite literal price to be paid. Dollars and Euros are exchanged with alacrity. Body form, clothing style, age, and health status are checked and monitored, and used to segregate and reject with impressive precision and speed. Women, particularly heterosexual women, are often present even as they risk being flattened out and packaged as idols or voyeurs, beings to focus the party and witness the politics of exclusion. What often passes as the LGBTQ community has been largely networked, and operates as a political and economic force that is thought to have grown past the grubbiness of porn theaters and toward the bright tomorrow of shopping sprees and companionate marriage. The good news, however, the shockingly good news, is that the whining, irritable, greedy, hungry, stinking, quick, patient, and cunning beast known as desire still remains untamed. It stalks, it cruises, it looks both left *and* right, it saddles up pleasant, alert, and appealing to the male, the female, the yellow, the brown, the black, the fat, the disabled, the clumsily dressed, the nappy-headed, the thick lipped, the hairy, the old, the clumsy, and the daring. And when it arrives, reeking of promise and invention, it whispers the same naughty word to those with enough temerity—and hope—to hear: contact!

Acknowledgments

I would like to thank Bill Bamberger of Bamberger Books, Robert S. Bravard of the Stevenson Library of Lock Haven University, Barbara Cruikshank of the Department of Political Science and Don Eric Levine of the Comparative Literature Department, both at the University of Massachusetts at Amherst, Peter Reinhardt of the Department of Political Science at Williams College, Jason Brenner and Robert Morales of Brooklyn, New York, Kenneth James of Brunswick, Maine, and Edward Summer of New York City for reading and commenting on earlier versions of this manuscript. Needless to say, errors, overstatements, and idiosyncrasies are all my own.

A small part of "Times Square Blue" first appeared under the title "X-X-X Marks the Spot," with photographs by Philip-Lorca diCorcia, in *Out Magazine,* December 1996–January 1997. The editors of New York University Press and I are deeply grateful to Philip-Lorca DiCorcia for permission to use here a number of his photographs that did not appear with the original article. His photographs appear on pages 9, 11, 13, 33, 59, 94, 105, 107, and 147. (All other photographs are by the author.)

A shorter version of ". . . Three, Two, One, Contact: Times Square Red" was delivered as the Annual Kessler Lecture at the Center for Lesbian and Gay Studies (CLAGS), SUNY Graduate Center, December 12, 1997. A slightly different version was presented as a Chancellor's Distinguished Faculty Lecture at the University of Massachusetts, April 15, 1998. The lecture will appear in *Giving Ground,* an anthology edited by Michael Sorkin and Joan Copjec (New York: Verso, 1999). My gratitude goes to the editors for allowing New York University Press to publish this expanded version.

Real names are used for all persons represented in the photographs, with their awareness and consent. In some of the anecdotes, I have adjusted names or other identifying elements to protect privacy.

—SRD

Writer's Preface

Times Square Red, Times Square Blue consists of two extended essays, a form I've grown quite fond of since my first try at it in 1974. In different ways, at different focal lengths, along different trajectories and at different intensities, both pieces look at aspects of New York City affected by the Times Square Development Project of the last few years.

A presupposition of both pieces is that New York City has anticipated and actively planned this redevelopment since the start of the sixties. The demolition proper that began along Forty-second Street in 1995 and the construction that will yield, among other things, four new office towers and several new entertainment centers along both sides of Forty-second Street between Seventh and Eighth Avenue by 2005, are a culmination of forty years' expectation and attendant real estate and business machinations, not to mention much concerted public disapproval and protest. The construction of World Wide Plaza at Fiftieth Street and Eighth Avenue during the mid-1980s and the destruction of more than half a dozen movie theaters along Eighth Avenue were as much a part of this process as what is now visibly happening at points along the Deuce—that strip of Forty-second Street that runs from Seventh to Eighth Avenue but (since it's never been formally defined) could be extended all the way to Ninth Avenue and even, say, as far as the Public Library just east of Bryant Park. In order to bring about this redevelopment, the city has instituted not only a violent reconfiguration of its own landscape but also a legal and moral revamping of its own discursive structures, changing laws about sex, health, and zoning, in the course of which it has been willing, and even anxious, to exploit everything from homophobia and AIDS to family values and fear of drugs.

Arguably it began March 15, 1961, when *New York Times* publisher Arthur Sudsberger sold Times Tower to signage mogul David Leigh, who stripped the building's ornamental stone and raised over its steel frame the Allied Chemical Building's blank walls. Within three years, the city published its first plans to obliterate the Deuce—with a convention center between Seventh and Eighth Avenues, running from Fortieth to Forty-third (moved west and south, it's today's Javits Center), through which Forty-second Street was to be a covered alley, like Forty-first Street today under Port Authority's joined buildings. Though it never came about, it began a freeze on property improvements. At Seventh and Broadway, the Metropolitan Opera House was already slated for demolition. In the same years I saw the Roxy in Greenwich Village closed up and torn down, where I'd gone regularly for gay sex in the back balcony, the stairways, and johns. In mid-April 1966 I returned from half a year in Europe. The talk was of a new TImes Square: It would bloom like Lincoln Center. Walk along the Deuce, though, and you felt the shabbier and shabbier theater fronts holding their breath. I was still well under thirty. Like many young people, I'd assumed the world—the physical reality of stores, restaurant locations, apartment buildings, and movie theaters and the kinds of people who lived in this or that neighborhood—was far more stable than it was. The changes I *had* seen were mostly in fashion, behavior, music, and attitude, while, save for a mandala or spirit-eye hung in a window, a psychedelic poster or colorful graffiti spread on a wall, the streets through which the burgeoning counterculture roamed remained much the same. But in the midst of that spurious vision of a stable world, it first struck me that "major redevelopment" of the Times Square area would mean *a priori* major demolition, destruction, and devastation in what had established itself not only in the American psyche, but in the international imagination, as one of the world's most famous urban areas. That fame hinged on an image of the illicit and the perverse as much as it hinged on a reputation for entertainment, for being a "film capital," and for serving as the focus of theatrical arts both for New York City and the United States, arts for which the area's central avenue—Broadway—was a metonym known worldwide.

As a black gay male who had first set off from Harlem for Times Square one Sunday morning in 1957, more than a decade prior to Stonewall, with the specific goal of coming out and who, since 1960, had regularly utilized those several institutional margins transversing the Forty-second Street area in which gay activity thrived, I had to acknowledge with that early newspaper announcement of redevelopment that an order of menace now hung over a goodly portion of the active aspect of my sexual life. That menace was quite apart from the homophobia manifested today in everything from the violences inflicted on the minds of gay men and women by religious leaders like the Reverend Falwell (who, within the month, I have watched on television claim he can "cure" homosexuality by bringing lesbians and gay men to Jesus), to the fatal violence meted out two weeks back on the beaten and broken body of Matthew Shepherd, bound to a fence on a cold Wyoming highway—not a full five months after the murder of James Byrd in Texas, dragged by a chain from the back of a truck for the crime of being black, and only days after pediatrician Barnett Slepian was shot to death in his home for performing abortions in western New York State. Certainly my own fairly calm material life in a world which nevertheless contains such violences (in a city where gay-bashing crimes are up by 80 percent this year) is the ground from which the thinking in these two pieces has grown.

As first conceived in October 1996, "Times Square Blue" purposed to look at the activity and people on the corner of Forty-second Street and Eighth Avenue, as well as glance at a few porn movie houses (which the city had caused to be permanently and finally boarded up only that month), and check out a couple of bars to the north on (or just off) Eighth Avenue.

"But what," asked a young woman editor, a reader of an early draft, "went on *in* those movie theaters, before they were closed? Let me see some of that."

It recalled a similar request from another young woman almost twenty-five years before. For answer, at first, I added a single paragraph. All the extensions of the piece since that version—almost seventy-five manuscript pages, which have become sections 2 through 6, and around which the earlier material now forms a sort of locative parergon—have grown from that one paragraph.

". . . Three, Two, One, Contact: Times Square Red" began as an invited academic lecture and, as such, launches itself with a different order of conceptual difficulty and employs a different level of rhetorical density. Its appeal to theoretical discourse, its mosaic structure, and its range of attendant topics make it as different from "Times Square Blue" as a piece roughly the same length and that (sometimes) focuses on similar topics can be. Indeed, all the commercial forces that yearn to reinstate those authorial unities of history, style, theory, and value are here at their most distressed, so that the very reasonableness of bringing the two together under paired titles in a single book is in question. But a few readers have suggested not so much that the two pieces are "good to think with" but rather that their very differences make them particularly productive for thinking *about* and *against* and *through each other*. If this is the case, their abutment, one against the other here, is worth it.

A commitment both to the vernacular and to the expert—and to combining them in reasonable and responsible ways—offers the reader a starting place from which she or he may, if inclined, begin to justify both the organizational eccentricities of "Times Square Red" (to name it by its subtitle) as well as the decision to publish two pieces of such different texture and structure in one book.

On my way to deliver some late revisions on the text to the managing editor at New York University Press, I stopped in to see a friend for half an hour at his book- , computer- , and memorabilia-crowded home. There I met a man who, when I mentioned the title of my book, told me he had worked for the Brandt theater chain on Forty-second Street up until 1984. That chain included the majority of the legitimate theaters there; the Brandt Theater itself was, by then, a porn house. The man erupted with a cascade of anecdotes about the appalling working conditions in the Forty-second Street theaters in those years, about young people hired at the concession stands for minimum wage (then $3.50 an hour) and still forced to join a company union as well as to testify in the company's favor at city hearings. All of this might easily and profitably be researched to expand the annals of human degradation. (Needless to say, most of these young people were black and Hispanic.) These tales are not told here—because, among other things, there *were* no concession stands in *any* of the porn theaters I write of. In this regard you will find here a passing concern for diachrony (the overall explanation for the situation the man described is certainly stated in the following pages), but neither "Times Square Blue" nor "Times Square Red" is a history of that area or the city.

Nor is either piece a plea to reinstate the porn theaters that the thoughtless greed running rampant in cities like New York has recently smashed. After all, such greed created those institutions at another moment. But even that greed is stabilized in its operations by attendant discourses. However indirect, my argument's polemical thrust is toward conceiving, organizing, and setting into place new establishments—and even entirely new types of institutions—that would offer the services and fulfill the social functions provided by the porn houses that encouraged sex among the audience. Further, such new institutions should make those services available not only to gay men but to all men and women, gay and straight, over an even wider social range than did the old ones.

This book is, then, an account, and in some passages an analysis, of how certain social surfaces functioned in interface with the men who paid a small price to utilize them (thirty-five cents in my earliest years at the Variety Photoplays theater, the 1960s, to five dollars at the Capri in the last months of 1995). That many of the things recounted are defensible and desirable is a product of certain ideologies (some of which are, yes, mine) and discourses (some of which I happily inhabit). Taken as a whole, the book is an attempt to dismantle some of those discourses, to analyze their material underpinnings, and to suggest ways they have changed over time—and thus to suggest ways you and I might further want to change them, unto continuing them at new sites and in new forms. The polemical passion here is forward-looking, not nostalgic, however respectful it is of a past we may find useful for grounding future possibilities.

Those familiar with studies of Pound's *Cantos* will be aware of Pound's use of the idea of the *periplum*—those early texts, from before the advent of universal latitude and longitude, that allowed the navigation of the Mediterranean from at least the Trojan War through classical and medieval times, even up through the era of Philip II and Elizabeth I. Periploi were detailed descriptions of the coastlines of the mainland and the various islands, which, when coupled with a bit of common sense about directions and travel times, allowed early navigators to ascertain where, after a storm, they might have ended up, once a coast came into view.

The dual pieces here present a sociological and diachronic periplum. They are two attempts by a single navigator to describe what the temporal coastline and the lay of the land looked like and felt like and the thoughts he had while observing them. From the most peremptory landings, these pieces register impressions and ideas as they occurred to this navigator, somewhat storm-tossed over thirty-odd years, who finally sought something no less necessary to his appetitive life than good food and fresh water.

From such impressions as these alone can anyone else decide whether it is worth going back and making a more historically concerned and concerted visit/invasion. Is there something there to research and learn from? Clearly I think there is. (Further investigation may well come up with a bunch of things *not* to do, if you want to establish such useful institutions.) But it is from those early impressions of what was visible along the coastline that others are most likely to decide whether or not they want to return and explore further.

The temporal coastline of the Forty-second Street/Eighth Avenue area is still changing in its material visibility weekly, monthly. The Venus Theater that figures in these pages is now the Daniella Pizzeria. The Eros I is now one of two Playwright Restaurants. (The Circus Theater over on Broadway has become another.) On the other side of the small parking lot, the Capri is now a restaurant called Starstruck.

The (old) Cats on Eighth Avenue gave way to a discount electronics store by 1992. Less than a year back, Ernie's boss sold off the Full Moon Saloon and the new owners gutted and remodeled it, discovering in the process a storeroom whose door had been sealed over—and in which there was nothing of interest. With its internal space bigger by that storeroom, now it's a bar called the Collins. Once again the Savoy is no longer gay; today it's a straight jazz bar, doing fairly well. Pretty much intact, the Savoy's funkier clientele moved to the new Cats, on Forty-eighth Street, where they settled in for about a year. Only a few weeks ago, however, *that* establishment closed.

Three months back, the neighborhood's adult video stores were forbidden to display their sexual material to the passing pedestrian public. Until recently their windows had been mosaics of colorful videocassette boxes, with pictures of naked women (and often a smaller window of naked men), blond and black and Asian. Now, with white or brown wrapping paper stuck up behind the glass, they look somewhere between comic and just weird. Many have grudgingly followed the city mandate to stock 60 percent minimum "family fare." One is reminded of seventeenth-century London and Marseille's response to the plague—though here the plague may just *be* that pleasant suburban couple, lawyer and doctor, herding their 2.3 children ahead of them, out the door of the airport van and into the Milford Plaza; or at least the family values, perhaps too easily, they might be taken by some to represent. But, the city has said to the video stores with Draconian finality, "Sixty percent—or get out." If the concern were actually for the morals of those 2.3 youngsters, it might be excusable. (Though streets such as these may, someday, feed their appetites, they do not *create* such appetites.) But it is only a continuation—or rather, the recent inflation—of policy that has ruled the neighborhood for three decades or more. Make any small business there as unprofitable as possible so that much bigger ones can buy them up cheaply, receive a certain amount of social approbation in the process, and proceed to replace them. If the city mandated that they had to stock 60 percent fresh fruit and put wrapping paper over *their* windows, it could put out of business most of the city's major department stores.

The Selwyn Theater—along with the Grand Luncheonette—was demolished over a year ago. The buildings pictured in the opening pages here, along the west extremity of the Deuce's north and south face, are gone. Though still incomplete as of this writing, the new construction already rises higher than ever those old buildings stood. At the east end, Ferrara's, Dapy, Magic Max, and Shade (mentioned in the first pages here as heralding the *new* Times Square) have only in the last months been boarded over, as *their* three-story building on the north west corner of Forty-second Street and Seventh Avenue (with its handsome Art Deco cornice, and containing yet *another* theater space, with its entrance on the avenue) is readied for demolition to make way for another of the fabled four towers.

In a lined denim jacket, with his stand set up on Eighth Avenue under a blue umbrella, Ben was out and working only last week. But any sort of inclemency in the weather, these days, keeps him in.

With the rush to accommodate the new, much that was beautiful along with much that was shoddy, much that was dilapidated with much that was pleasurable, much that was inefficient with much that was functional, is gone. The idea that all that is going was ugly and awful is as absurd as it would be to propose that what was there was only of *any* one moral color. What was there was a complex of interlocking systems and subsystems. Precisely at the level where the public could avail itself of the neighborhood, some of those subsystems were surprisingly beneficent—beneficent in ways that will be lost permanently unless people report on their own contact and experience with those subsystems.

I hope these two extended essays function as early steps (though by no means are they the first) in thinking through the problem of where people, male and female, gay and straight, old and young, working class and middle class, Asian and Hispanic, black and other, rural and urban, tourist and indigene, transient and permanent, with their bodily, material, sexual, and emotional needs, might discover (and even work to set up) varied and welcoming harbors for landing on our richly variegated urban shore.

Part 1

Times Square Blue

October 1996

The great epochs of our life are where we win the courage to rechristen our
evil as what is best in us.

—NIETZSCHE, *Beyond Good and Evil,* §116

I

Against the subway kiosk around the corner on Forty-second Street and Eighth Avenue, Ben still sets up his shoeshine stand, his bottles of polish and cans of stain,
his brushes and cloths. Ben's come-on is much what it was when I first noticed him
in the late seventies. For every third or fourth woman in the passing bustle, with
or without a boyfriend, it's "Hey, *there,* beautiful!" or "*Mmmm!* Hi, *sweetheart!*"
There's never an obscenity or mention of a bodily part, other than perhaps "*Umm,*
that's *nice!*" or "Honey, you are *somethin'!*" But the hailing is clear and the inflec-
tion is drenched enough in both sensuality and sexuality to startle practically anyone, especially the white women with even a bit of naïveté left—or the men with
them, who are really Ben's mark, though anyone in leather shoes will do. Who
does—who *could*—this black guy think he's talking to like that? For when, surprised, woman or boyfriend turns, the head lifts, or the eyes look up, Ben—so
faintly, and within the beat—shifts his tone from pander to preacher: "You are a
truly *fine* woman, and it's a pleasure to see you pass on the street! I'm so glad
there're women like you out today!" or "Sir, you have a beautiful woman there.
You're a lucky man. Respect her and treat her well!" Now people smile—men *and*

Looking west along the south side of Forty-second Street between Seventh and Eighth Avenues, beneath the marquee of another condemned movie theater.

women. (Maybe one in five—the women in groups or the single ones—doesn't smile.) But it's harmless, even charming, isn't it? In his shorts and his sunglasses for Indian summer, he's just this old black shoeshine man—who makes enough shining shoes so that pretty much annually he and his wife can fly over to spend the Christmas holidays with her family in Germany. "If the women smile, see, then the men *gotta* get their shoes shined, to show that they're good sports and that they go along with it; *and* to put me back in my place just a little. It's a game we play. That's all. I got friends from all over the world that I made out here. People come back here every year, just to take their picture with me!"

For all the years I've watched others smile and smiled with them, something troubles me in all this. (Ben gives his age as seventy-two; but his hair's still black. Most people wouldn't put him at sixty.) It isn't Ben. Back and forth over the bound-

ary between unacceptable harassments and protestations of admiration, sometimes three or four times a minute, his agile leaps are a virtuoso performance by an
astute observer of the streets (one moment leering fondly down at the prostitute
ambling along the gutter and, an instant on, gazing with articulate awe up at the
pedestal on which his interpellation has replaced her so quickly that the ride is, for
her, even as it's over, a moment on the city's cultural Tilt-a-Whirl), and on a street
that can boast of being the most famous in America: Forty-second Street.

What bothers me in Ben's routine is where the boundary sits. Ben didn't put
it there. But does his witty and always slightly disorienting performance help erase
it? Or does that performance inscribe it more deeply? Honestly, I can't tell. Perhaps
it does some of both. Let's go around the corner.

In these autumn days of September and October, for those who recall the
Deuce from even two or three years ago, walking along Forty-second Street from
Eighth to Seventh Avenue is an odd experience. Once, more than half a dozen
movie houses ran till near eleven P.M. Till ten, selling cameras, boom boxes, calculators, phone-answering machines, faxes, and camcorders, guys lingering in the
glass doorways would ask you what you were looking for. When you stopped at the
window, they'd cajole, "No, come on in! Come in. Come on inside. We've got it
for you!"

Fast-food joints alternated with flashy clothing stores. On display dummies,
striped, black, or polka-dotted fare sported gold chains and purple handkerchiefs
blooming from breast pockets. In the middle of the block was Modell's Sporting
Goods. Toward the Eighth Avenue end, sandwiched between the subway arcade
and the Georgia Chicken Kitchen, a mini-grocery sold sodas and beer at only a
dime per can more than you'd pay around the corner.

Today they're gone. Even the Jennie Holzer haikus that, for a season, deco-
rated the silent marquees ("All art is either / revolution / or plagiarism"; "In
Greenwich Village / a tourist asks directions / to Greenwich Village") and the
theater fronts turned into mournfully playful art (behind the glass doors of one,

5

Standing just in from Eighth Avenue, at about eleven in the morning, September 25, 1996, looking east along Forty-second Street's north face. Metal gates, painted orange, red, purple, and yellow, are down in front of the vacated stores, in preparation for demolition, which will start in a few months. Most of the stores here sold radios, calculators, camcorders, and electronic gadgets. At least one sold secondhand men's magazines. The marquee of the Harem, a porn theater for more than a decade and scheduled for destruction, is visible to the right, just west of Modell's Sporting Goods.

under little spotlights, shoes fixed to the floor led off between diaphanous white gowns; at another, in the display window a video projection of a huge red mouth lipped vaguely suggestive phrases: "I've got it for you. Come here, this is it. Here it is, what you're looking for") have been dismantled. Painted purple, orange, blue, and red, corrugated metal gates are down over all the storefronts from the block's west end to . . . well, to about the three-quarters point. After that, there's the New Victory Children's Theater, just opened, its pyramidal entrance jutting into the sidewalk's center. Already, east of the New Victory, across from the Disney Store, glass and gray facades striped with red and blue neon hint at Times Square's new look. On the corner of Seventh, Ferarra's sells coffee and pastry; Shade sells (of course) sunglasses and sun hats; and Dapy proffers a variety of tourist junk. On the other side of the street, the largest theater on the strip, the New Amsterdam, is currently being gutted. This is the work of the Forty-second Street Development Project, the best-known and most visible member of which is the Walt Disney Company.

From eight-thirty to ten-thirty A.M. and, back the other way, from four-thirty to six-thirty P.M., thousands on thousands of working men and women pour across it. The rest of the time, today, it's all but empty. A four-stool hot dog and knish stand still holds on under the right side of the Selwyn Theater marquee: the Grand Luncheonette. There over half a century, maybe it's got another year. Across the street, office workers are still in and out of the twenty-three-story Candler Building. But the guys in their tank tops and baseball caps who used to hang out toward the Eighth Avenue end, in front of Ben's portable stand, walking up beside you as you pass (*sotto voce*: "Loose joints, Valium, black beauties . . . 'Ludes . . . Sen'similla . . ." or whatever was going on the street that day), are gone.

Across the avenue, diagonally south of Ben's corner, Anthony Campbell has worked as a taxi dispatcher at the Port Authority for ten years. At the curbside booth on the southwest corner of Forty-second Street and Eighth, just under the Port's girdered marquee, sometimes he sits, sometimes he stands. Over pedestrian and car traffic noise, he shouts at the taxis, calls to the passengers: "Come on, right here! Yeah! That one—take *that* one." In slow stretches, he can conduct things from his stool inside his booth. During heavy traffic hours, he's up in the street and striding about, his gesturings and signalings providing him an aerobic workout. At the curb, the yellow cab file gets longer or shorter. Behind the chains, the passenger line lengthens and contracts. Has the shutting down of Forty-second Street

Established sometime around World War II, selling hot dogs, hamburgers, coffee, and knishes, the Grand Luncheonette operated under the right side of the Selwyn Theater marquee on the north face of Forty-second Street between Seventh and Eighth Avenues. It would be demolished when the Selwyn was pulled down.

changed the amount of taxi business? Campbell hesitated a moment, then spoke slowly and thoughtfully. "No, not really." Well, has it changed the kind of people he gets cabs for? "No. It hasn't. There're not many changes so far." What changes did he see for the future? "There may be some when it's finished, once they get the new movies in."

What Campbell's uninflected observations index is the consistency to the traffic in and out of the Port. The vast majority of that traffic is working folk who have to hoof it, morning and evening, across the strip or up and down Eighth Avenue to get to their job. Part of it is made up, yes, of tourists on their week or weekend in the city with a night or two at a Broadway show. But, at least at the taxi-taking level, they're not the indigenous New Yorkers who used to come in on subway, city bus, or foot to see the movies or to buy from the electronics shops that dominated that so-famous block running off it to the east.

I stepped from the taxi dispatcher's booth to one of the vendors, Christos, a stocky southern Mediterranean with a walrus mustache. I've been buying shish kebabs from his covered aluminum cart for a decade now. His meat is good. His licenses are up to date. Asking him the same questions I'd asked Mr. Campbell, I got much the same answers. But tell me, I persisted, what kind of people do you see out here on the corner?

Christos grinned. "*You* know the kind of people who hang out around here."

Taxi dispatcher Anthony Campbell stands by a dispatcher's booth at the Port Authority, while a workmate sits, as cabs pull up to the curb.

A shish kebab wagon stands at the southwest corner of Forty-second Street and Eighth Avenue, on the corner of the Port Authority bus station.

Sometimes you'll find Darrell Deckard on that corner—a *good*-looking black man of twenty-six. Mother from Missouri, father from Georgia, Darrell (if you look in his direction long enough, and no cops are around) might reach between the legs of his baggy black jeans and casually squeeze his crotch in a way that could mean he was just scratching, but that also shows what's under the denim. If you smile, he might smile back, come over, and start a conversation. What's he doing out here?

"I'm a hustler, man. What do you think I do?" Darrell is friendly, straightforward, sharp, and doesn't beat around the bush. "Who's got time for that? I'm out here sellin' it, man, to make me some money! How long have I been here . . . ? I've been working out here about two years." What changes has Darrell seen since the Deuce closed down? "*More* police; and *less* money! People be scared now, you know

Forty-second Street hustlers Darrell Deckard and David Rosenbloom take a few minutes out from work, to sit by a parking lot wall near Ninth Avenue.

what I'm sayin'? They stay home. Makes you wanna get a regular job. They be hustlers out now, but they can't stay in one place." (Darrell excused himself to help a guy having beeper trouble. A minute later he was back, after a quick confab with one of his regulars—a middle-aged black man in a white sweatshirt, white gym pants, and white cap, with gold-rimmed granny glasses.) "See, they got cops hidin' in all the peep shows. They got the Public Morals Squad out here—whatever the fuck that means." As we strolled half a block west to a parking lot in which to take his picture, Darrell collared a white friend, Dave—shorter, leaner, scruffier (and Dave's eyes don't look in quite the same direction): "Hey, man—run up there for me, and tell my guy that I'll be back in a few minutes." Which guy, Dave wanted to know. "Go on, man! Go on—*you* know who he is. You've seen me with him before." So Dave ran off—and was back in five.

Darrell demanded: "Did you tell 'im?"

"I told *somebody*!" Dave explained.

Twenty-eight, Dave hustles too. While we set up our camera, Darrell and Dave mimed karate moves at one another and joked about the specific sexual services each sold. At one point Darrell broke up. "Man, that nigger wants a hit of crack *so* bad . . . I stopped smoking it, myself, last week. But that nigger—" meaning very white Dave—"will do *anything* for his hit!" Anything, here, meant sitting down to let himself be photographed too, for the fifteen dollars we offered him for his time and his signature on the model release. Then Dave was *gone*!

What changes did Darrell see coming, once the renovations were complete? "You just have to wait, man. See what happens, know what I'm sayin'? There's no way to tell."

I cited what another young man had told me only a week ago on the same corner: Isn't everything moving to Thirty-fourth Street, with the action going into the peep shows down there?

"No, man—that was before! This week the cops have been cracking down on people even there! That's why I'm up *here*." As we returned to the Eighth Avenue corner, Darrell looked around for his regular. "He must have found someone else. Well, I know him. He'll be back. I'll get 'im next time, don't worry!" Darrell was off into the crowd.

As I got ready to stroll north, a dark hand fell on my shoulder. "Hey, man—upstairs, in the rest rooms?" It's a scrawny, wholly unexceptional looking black man in his late thirties named Jeff. On the street, other than to note that he's probably homeless, you wouldn't give him a second look. In a public rest room, at Penn Station or at Port Authority, however, when he stands before a urinal, slouched a leisurely eight to ten inches back from the porcelain fixture, I've never seen anyone *not* at least glance in his direction—astonished, with opened mouth and blinking eyes. "They got the cops hidin' in the booths, looking out at

Darrell Deckard on Forty-second Street.

what goes on—or holin' up in the service closets, looking through the slit in the door. Pulled me in twice last week. So you watch out there, now. Just thought you'd wanna know . . ."

"Thanks, Jeff . . ."

He shambled south.

For those interested in hard-edged figures: Darrell asks forty or fifty but will sneak into a peep show booth with you long enough for one of you to come for twenty—and he's a very busy man. Jeff starts at twenty—and he probably makes a more consistent living.

The nostalgic approach sees all these silent red and green and purple window gates, these dead and wordless movie marquees, as the end of an era, marked by the dispersal of so many of the sexual businesses we haven't really mentioned yet. It's been a licentious and lively area since before the *New York Times* moved into

Times Tower and, in 1904, persuaded the city to change the name from Longacre Square, before, in 1912, transferring to its current Forty-third Street location. An acquaintance with New York's history suggests, however, that we are not so much at an end. Rather, we're at the midpoint in a process parts of the city have undergone many times. Its fundamental principle was articulated succinctly by former police chief William McAdoo in 1906 (a year after Anthony Comstock shut down George Bernard Shaw's *Mrs. Warren's Profession* on Broadway and a year before he forced Richard Strauss's *Salomé* to close at the Met, both after a single performance): "As everyone knows, the city is being rebuilt, and vice moves ahead of business."

The opening of the old Metropolitan Opera House at Broadway and Seventh Avenue in 1883 first brought vice up from Mercer Street and the lower parts of Greenwich Village, where the rising rents were driving out the houses of prostitution, so that only industrial businesses could afford those downtown locations. In 1889 court testimony revealed that Nathan Niles, then president of the Tradesmen's National Bank, owned a brothel on West Forty-third Street, run by the "French Madame," Elize Purret. The same year the *Times* came, 1904, the Interborough Rapid Transit opened the subway system, with its nickel fare (no tokens—or metrocards—back then) that lasted into the fifties. Feeding into the city just to its west, with *its* opening in 1937, the Lincoln Tunnel only added to the value. With a smaller version first swinging wide its doors in 1950, the now block-long pair of Port Authority buildings simply assured that this would be the city's incoming traffic center for years. With the theater district to the north and its central location on Manhattan Island, it was a developer's dream.

And the vice?

It was peep shows, sex shops, adult video stores and dirty magazine stores, massage parlors—and porn theaters. A few years ago there were two on the east end of the block's north side, one at the block's west end, and another across the street, with some seven scattered up and down Eighth Avenue, from the Cameo at Forty-fourth to the Adonis at Fifty-first, as well as a flourishing trade in female street-walkers, drugs, and hustlers.

The threat from AIDS produced a 1985 health ordinance that began the shut-down of the specifically gay sexual outlets in the neighborhood: the gay movie houses and the straight porn theaters that allowed open masturbation and fellatio in the audience. For a dollar forty-nine in the seventies, and for five dollars in the year before they were closed (several less than twelve months ago), from ten in the morning till midnight you could enter and, in the sagging seats, watch a projection of two or three hard-core pornographic videos. A few trips up and down the aisle while your eyes got accustomed to the darkness revealed men sitting off in the shadows—or, sometimes, full out under the occasional wall lights—masturbating . . . if someone hadn't stood up on the seat and unscrewed the bulb. Sit a seat away from one, and you would either be told to go away, usually fairly quietly, or invited to move closer (if only by the guy's feigned indifference). Should he be one of *your* regulars, you might even get a grin of recognition.

Occasionally men expected money—but most often, not. Many encounters were wordless. Now and again, though, one would blossom into a conversation lasting hours, especially with those men less well-off, the out-of-work, or the homeless with nowhere else to go.

In the sixties I found similar theaters in every capital of Europe. That may explain why foreign gay tourists located these places here so quickly. The population was incredibly heterogeneous—white, black, Hispanic, Asian, Indian, Native American, and a variety of Pacific Islanders. In the Forty-second Street area's sex theaters specifically, since I started frequenting them in the summer of 1975, I've met playwrights, carpenters, opera singers, telephone repair men, stockbrokers, guys on welfare, guys with trust funds, guys on crutches, on walkers, in wheelchairs, teachers, warehouse workers, male nurses, fancy chefs, guys who worked at Dunkin Donuts, guys who gave out flyers on street corners, guys who drove garbage trucks, and guys who washed windows on the Empire State Building. As a gentile, I note

15

that this is the only place in a lifetime's New York residency I've had any extended conversation with some of the city's Hasidim. On a rainy Friday in 1977 in one such theater, the Variety, down on Third Avenue just below Fourteenth Street, I met a man who became my lover for eight years. My current lover (with whom I've lived happily for going on seven), once we'd met, discovered we'd both patronized the Capri, only we'd never encountered each other because I usually went in the day, while he always went at night. Once we began to live with one another, we often visited the theater together—till it was closed, toward the start of this year. There are many men, younger and older, for whom the ease and availability of sex there made the movies a central sexual outlet.

Nostalgia presupposes an uncritical confusion between the first, the best, and the youthful gaze (through which we view the first and the best) with which we create origins. But the transformation from the cheap Village, Delancey Street, Fourteenth Street, Upper West Side, and (supremely) Forty-second Street movie theaters of the fifties and sixties (where you could generally find some sort of sexual activity in the back balcony, off to the side, or in the rest rooms) to the porn theaters of the seventies (a number of them set up specifically for quick, convenient encounters among men) does not, in my memory at any rate, fit easily into such an originary/nostalgic schema.

By the early seventies the movie industry was already reeling under the advent of home video technology. Suddenly it became impossible to fill up the larger theatrical spaces that had attracted audiences since before the Depression, eager to see this or that new celluloid epic, that or this new double feature.

All over the country, save for a few major venues (in New York the Ziegfeld, the Astor Plaza) that persevered like filmic museums from another era, movie theaters underwent an almost spontaneous mitosis—dividing into two, three, four, and even six viewing spaces. The film of Ray Bradbury's *Something Wicked This Way Comes* (1983) was probably the last movie I watched from a full-sized neighborhood theater balcony before, a season later, a tetraplex took over the space and, a season after that, at Broadway and Eighty-third Street, a hexplex opened next door on the same block, so that briefly in my neighborhood we had a choice of *ten* films at any one time, where three years before there had been only one. And around the Forty-second Street area a decade or more of idle speculation on the renovation of the Times Square area ("Movie Capital of the World," as it billed itself on the wall sign over the upper floors of the Forty-second Street Apollo—not to be confused with the Harlem house of the same name and greater notoriety) turned into active plans and active buying—and/or an active freeze on all real improvements, since the whole thing would be bought up and pulled down in a year or more, wouldn't it . . . ?

Under this economic pressure in the early-to-middle seventies, some two dozen small theaters were given over as outlets for the nascent pornographic film industry: a handful between Sixth Avenue and Eighth Avenue along Forty-second Street proper, another handful on Broadway (the Circus, the Big Apple, the Baby Doll . . .), and another half dozen or so up along Eighth, starting with the Cameo on the west side of the avenue between Forty-third and Forty-fourth and running up to the Adonis. Most of the theaters purveyed straight fare, but a few (the Adonis, the Eros I and II, the King, the David, the Bijoux, and, in later years, one half of the Hollywood) provided gay features. The transformation meant that from then on all major repairs for these properties were at an end. Only those without which the theaters could not stay open were done. In that condition the porn theaters continued, not for two, three, or four years, but for the next twenty-five. Some did not last the duration. Each new burst of interest in the area's renovation would be accompanied by a new wave of do-gooder rhetoric, and a theater or two would go. By the middle eighties the three houses between Sixth and Seventh were gone. One on the north side had been turned into a fried chicken emporium. Another had become a sporting goods store. The Bryant (that had featured "Live Sex Shows," which, at five performances a day between ten and ten, were exactly that: a brown or black couple spent twenty minutes on a bare blue-lit stage, first the woman stripping for the man, then fellating him, then his performing cunnilingus on her, and finally the two of them screwing in two or three positions, finishing—with pull-out orgasms for a few of the after-six shows—to polite applause from the largely forty-plus male audience, before the porn film started once more. At the back of the chest-high wall behind the last row of orchestra seats, usually some guy would give you a hand job or sometimes a blow job; there for a couple of weeks I gave my quota of both) was simply a south-side vacant lot.

Perhaps the biggest event in that twenty-five- or thirty-year history was when, around 1986, the last thirty-five-millimeter projector ceased to roll in the projection rooms of the Capri, the Venus, the Harem, the Sweetheart, and the Hollywood, to be replaced by often blurry, out of focus, pale, flickering three-color video projectors. Such projectors had already been installed in the gay theaters—the King, the David, and the Bijoux down on Third Avenue, just below Variety Photoplays. In the middle eighties the Variety still alternated a porn film with a legit movie throughout the day for an entrance price of $2.50, just up from $1.95 a year back, and $1.45 a year before that. ("We apologize to our patrons for the raise in price," read the cardboard sign hung inside the ticket window. "But face it: Even at $2.50 we're still a bargain.") But everywhere else the video industry that had precipitated the change had finally triumphed—practically without a ripple.

The earliest years in those theaters (i.e., the first half of the pre-video years, prior to 1980) were a time of what now seem like quite extraordinary experiments: the porn theater where, for example, every other seat was removed, the ones remaining making a ghostly checkerboard of the orchestra—on the assumption that the stereotyped "furtive businessmen" with overcoats draped across their laps, which various *Playboy* and even *New Yorker* cartoons presented as the utilizer of the facilities, would appreciate as much room as possible between each seat and the next.

Six months later, the missing seats were back.

Furtive businessmen were just not the audience in these places. The guys who wandered in were working stiffs—the ones who came during the day, between jobs or on their day-off—most from age twenty-five to fifty, but with an extensive flattening of the bell curve at either end.

Here are some memories from the earliest days of the commercial porn houses, when mores and manners—largely based on those of movie cruising before the porn films proper came in—were still being established.

II

At the Variety Photoplays you gave the elderly fellow inside his booth your dollar, and, through the tiny window in the glass, he gave you a nickel change and your ticket from a large roll—weekdays yellow, Saturdays orange, Sundays blue. (Yes, it was 95¢ in the seventies, up from 45¢ in the sixties.) Always in a brown or blue suit and a red bow tie, he mumbled heatedly to himself nonstop. For years the theater had been a gay sexual cruising ground. The (strictly heterosexual) pornographic movies started as a Saturday offering. At first management was afraid the straight films might drive away the theater's gay audience. The tickets' color coding allowed them to compare the take from days when sex films played and days when legit features ran. The figures for the porn were pretty good, however. Soon it was pornography Tuesdays, Thursdays, and Saturdays, with legit films the other days. Within a year and a half, it was double-feature porn Monday through Saturday. On Sunday, in deference to what I'll never know, a porn film alternated with a legit offering. That persisted for another year, till the porn drove out even that.

Finally all the tickets were yellow.

If anything, the gay activity increased.

You went in through glass doors, where a guy leaned from his stool and ripped your ticket in half. Weekends, from the time the theater opened at ten till four or five in the afternoon, three Puerto Ricans managed the house. With muscled arms, a brutal face, and shiny hair, the youngest, in his late thirties, sat on the stool and tore tickets, without interrupting his machine gun chatter. With a silver mane, the oldest usually wore a gym suit and sandals. Sometimes he spelled the youngest on the stool. Other times, he stood around, telling stories of his pimping days. Between them in age, a heavy fellow lounged with them (he always wore a cap), an audience for the complaints of the youngest and the boasts of the eldest. Their conversation listed from English to Spanish to English, from argument to laughter and back.

When, after two years in England, I came down from my first university teaching job in Buffalo and started going again to the Variety in the summer of '75, I assumed all three men were straight. Later I decided the heavy one was a gay friend of the other two. Easily, though, I could have been wrong on any count.

Refrequenting the Variety (I'd gone there often before going abroad), I noticed a dozen or so patrons were men I'd seen there regularly three, five, ten years before. The place seemed almost a kind of family, with a neighborhood feel—though men came there from as far as the Bronx, Queens, Westchester, or (a tree service worker and his uncle) Brewster, New York.

It was surprising how little the pornography changed that.

One day, in the Variety's balcony, I noticed a good-looking Spanish guy in his early twenties—possibly even his late teens, sitting in the forward seats to the left. At least eight months of roof-top weight lifting had filled out his orange T-shirt's shoulders. He'd opened his khaki pants and was masturbating. As I watched, an older guy moved into the seat beside him, leaned close, and whispered. Pausing the length of two or three strokes, the younger guy said something back. The older rose and moved away, while the kid went back to what he was doing.

Over the next twenty minutes two more men sat next to him. To each he said something. Again, each left—one to sit two seats away, the other to wander off into the theater's black.

Pretty soon, no one was joining him any more. The young man went on energetically pumping at himself, a seat free on either side. Later, in the "lounge"—what the longer-term customers called the space behind a small wall backing the balcony's last row, under a filthy skylight—I overheard two men, one black, one white:

"That straight kid over there—beating off? He's gorgeous. Why isn't anybody doing him?"

"Oh, he tells anybody who sits beside him he wants to do it himself. He says you can watch, but he wants you to sit at least a seat away."

"*Oh*—I *see!* Well, I just don't know if my heart could stand that. I'll go downstairs and let him do his thing."

One or the other chuckled in the theater's shadow.

Awhile later, walking along the horizontal aisle between the balcony's front and back seats, I glanced at the young guy, two rows below and a few seats to the side, when suddenly he put back his head, black hair glimmering in the screen's light in rhythm with his fist. He blinked twice, closed his eyes, clamped his teeth, and, as his lips pulled apart, in two large gouts and a smaller, from his speeding grip his fluids arched into the black between his khaki knees, wide against two different seat backs. Jerkily his fist slowed—and he growled.

After moments, breathing hard, he sat up to grin. "Hey . . . that was a . . . pretty good one, wasn't it?"

Left and right from three and four seats away, half a dozen men looked at him and grinned back—as a forty-year-old Asian man, somewhat heavy, in a suit jacket and sitting a row behind him, caught his breath and, only a bit less spectacularly, came.

The young man looked up and—still grinning—saw me: "Not bad—hey, you're watchin' me too?"

I nodded.

"I'm gettin' off on her up there—" he pointed at the screen—"and you guys are all gettin' off on *me* . . . ? That's funny, huh? That guy there—" His hand swung to point to the Asian—"he *always* comes the same time I do. Don't you? Didn't you? Come on—didn't you?" He looked back at me. "He always does that. Every time. I shoot—*he* shoots. Ain't that a trip?" Looking over, he laughed.

Smiling somewhat sheepishly, the Asian glanced up at me.

"That's really funny, huh?" the guy went on volubly. "I don't mind, though. It ain't nothin'." Turning back to the screen, he made two fists, stretched his arms wide, and yawned. "Well, I'm gonna get off a couple more times—" he glanced at his watch—"Damn! I been here since this place opened—then I'm goin' home."

I wandered away. But ten minutes later, when I walked by again, I looked down over the rail to see him once more industriously at work. Some of the guys around him had gone. Some new ones had sat down to observe.

My own adventures kept me in the orchestra, so that an hour and a half later when, thinking of leaving, I wandered into the lobby, as I looked away from the ticket taker arguing on his stool with his two friends, up the stairway to the balcony along the lobby's wall by the movie posters, in his orange T-shirt and khaki slacks, the same young man ambled lackadaisically down. When he was a third of the way, however, I saw—with some shock—his fly was open. His uncut penis, along with both testicles, hung free.

The sight of genitals when you don't expect them—in a public space, say— astonishes. The heart pounds. The stomach clutches. This is what makes exposure a violation. But it is not the greatest astonishment in the world. And acclimation mitigates it.

For a moment I wondered if, indeed, it was oversight. (And when we are astonished, we often laugh; which is healthy, if the shock signals no danger.) Just then, among the three men at the door, the heavy one in the baseball cap looked up. With a slightly suspended smile, he turned to the others. "Hey—there's your cousin up there." And laughed.

The guy on the stool looked—and suddenly frowned. "Hey, what the fuck you doin'?"

Disingenuously, the guy coming down the steps glanced over. "What do you mean . . . ?"

"Come on, man—put yourself away, now!"

"Huh?" the guy persisted, though a smile was trying to fight its way out from behind his nonchalance.

"Come on—now. Put your fuckin' dick away! You hear me?"

Glancing down at himself, the guy feigned bemusement. "Huh? My *cock*—why? What's the matter with it?"

"It's out your damned pants! *That's* what's wrong with it. Damn it," the ticket taker said, "I ain't gonna let you in here no more if you don't—"

"Why do I gotta put *my* dick away?" The young man came down another step. "Everybody in the movie's got his dick out his pants, beatin' off. Or somebody suckin' on him. Or *something*—"

"Look—" the guy got off his stool now and gestured—"people can see you, man. From outside. Come *on*, now!"

The kid on the stairs broke out laughing and, finally, pushed his privates back in his slacks. Zipping up, he came on into the lobby.

"You're crazy," his older cousin repeated. "You do that again and I won't let you come in here no more—"

"I'm *not* crazy," the younger guy said. "I'm havin' fun. That's what everybody does here. You said so—what, *you* don't go in there and do it too sometimes? You *told* me you did—"

"Not where everybody can *see*—"

"Why not? That's what everybody *else* does."

The other two were grinning, of course. But, past its emotional peak, the conversation slid along its developmental slope into Spanish, now that the phallic display was again veiled. The kid came over to stand in the door with them while they talked of something else.

A week or two later, when I was again in the Variety's balcony, again I looked over the rail to see the guy was back—in about the same seat. That day I'd brought in three cans of ginger ale. After drinking one, I decided I was going to leave early.

"Hey," I called down over the rail, where he was sitting, pants open, but for the moment only holding himself in his fist, "you want a soda? I'm going to leave soon, and I don't want to carry these around with me."

He looked up. "Huh? Oh, yeah—thanks, man." He took the can I held down to him.

Still leaning on the rail, I asked, "Your cousin downstairs decided to let you back in?"

He frowned, then realized what I must have been talking about. "Oh, yeah, he lets me in for nothin'. He's a good guy."

"You like it?"

Again he considered. "Yeah, it's okay. Guys don't crowd you here—I mean, if you ask them to leave you alone. Sometimes you got to tell 'em, you know, move over. I don't like that, somebody sitting right next to me while I'm beatin' my meat. I mean, I don't want no blow job or nothin'. Some guys here, they like that, but that's just not my thing. You wanna sit around and watch, I don't give a fuck about that. I mean, sure, sometimes, guys *stare*—you know. I don't like *that*, either. You know, just *staring*—" Opening his eyes wide, he thrust his head forward in an imitation of an overcurious observer. "But these guys are okay." He looked around at the other men a seat, a row, or three seats away. (Two glanced at him. One smiled.) "It's better than those places uptown, you know, where they come around and shine a fuckin' flashlight on you—scare you to *death* up there! I mean, you're beatin' off—and suddenly you got this *flashlight* in your face! No, this is nice here.

These guys in here, they're nice." He gestured with the can I'd given him. "Hey, thanks for the soda, man." Turning back around, he opened the tab, drank, sat it on the floor—and, among the half a dozen in their seats about him (including, I saw once more, the Asian from last week), fell to his rhythmic work.

The above would seem to require that someone point out vigorously (and with differing contents our literature is full of such all-male scenes, similarly structured) that its charm, sociality, and warmth—if it has any—depend entirely on the absence of "the woman"—or at least depend on flattening "the woman" till she is only an image on a screen, whether of light or memory, reduced to "pure" "sexuality," till, a magical essence, a mystical energy, she pervades, grounds, even fuels the entire process, from which she is corporally, intellectually, emotionally, and politically absent.

I was describing to a friend this evidently straight man, his openness to the gay men around him, his humorous exhibitionism, when suddenly she said, "I want to *see* some of that—and all the sex you're talking about that goes on, too!"

A voracious reader with short dark hair, and a stocky little Hispanic woman, Ana did office temp work during the day; by night she was a wonderfully talented guitarist and singer, working in the small clubs around the Village. "Would you ever take me . . . with you?"

"It's dark in there." I laughed. "You'd have to squint—at least till your eyes adjusted."

"What *would* happen if you took a woman in there?" she went on. "Probably everybody would get all upset and angry—"

"I don't think so," I said. "Couples come in sometimes. Mostly, that's guys with prostitutes. But not always. About the worst thing that happens is that some fellow will sit a seat away from you and beat off."

"That," she said, "I think I could handle."

One Thursday afternoon (on purpose I chose a time when it wasn't too crowded) I took Ana not to the Variety but to the Metropolitan, another porn theater further east on Fourteenth Street. I wore jeans, a red-checked shirt, and contact lenses. Ana wore jeans, a man's white shirt, a denim jacket, and her thick, pink-rimmed glasses. We hadn't discussed costumes, but I thought, for a first-time visit, she'd made a wiser choice . . . than, say, heels, miniskirt, and beaded halter.

Somewhat larger than the Variety, the Metropolitan was set up differently. A horseshoe balcony ran around its second level. The walls were painted black. (The Variety's were dark blue.) Several stairways led up and down, and thus there was a good deal more traffic between levels, which somehow seemed a positive factor for taking someone unfamiliar with the place—and who would be perceived, certainly, as an unfamiliar visitor.

When we paid our entrance fee and stepped in, the Greek manager suddenly stepped up and took my forearm—so that, at first not noticing, Ana walked on ahead. "If I hear she's takin' any money, man," he said to me in a heavy accent, "I'm gonna throw you *both* out! This ain't no whorehouse."

Somewhat startled, I said, "Oh—don't worry!"

Patting my arm, he went on in a more explanatory tone: "'Cause the pimps bring women in here, and try to turn tricks right in the movie. I can't have that going on. I mean, this is a nice place. People come in here to have fun, not to pay no whores."

"Yeah, sure," I said. And pulled away to catch up with Ana.

"What was that about?" she asked.

I told her. She laughed.

Though it had a double door making a narrow vestibule, like many theater buildings dating from before World War I, the Metropolitan had no real lobby.

"When I come in here," I said, as we moved behind the final row of seats, through the reddish light at the back of the orchestra, "I usually take a quick tour of the whole place, just to see how things are looking. Here, that's down the aisle there and up that one over there. Then it's once around the balcony—"

She said: "Go on."

So I did, with Ana behind.

When we finished our round of the orchestra and left the ground floor to walk up the steps to the balcony, I asked her, "How many guys did you see giving other guys head, downstairs?"

"Huh?" she said.

"I saw three."

"Come on, not right out in the middle of the . . . oh, you're kidding me—"

Just then two black kids dashed down the steps beside us. One glanced at Ana and whispered, "Uh-oh . . . fish!" "Fish" was gay slang for women. But I don't think it registered with Ana—or, indeed, just then, with his friend two steps below.

We came out at one end of the horseshoe, to walk up beside the double pairs of seats, mostly empty. On my first circuit, I saw a thickset man in workmen's greens, sitting by the balcony rail and gazing at the screen, an empty seat beside him. In his late thirties (older, then, than Ana or I), he'd opened his pants and was fingering himself absently.

At least a decade his senior, a slender man leaned by the wall, watching. In white shirt and dark vest, he stepped away to move toward the seated workman— as we passed.

Continuing with me to the back, Ana commented softly, "There *are* a lot of people in here walking around . . ." There were. But since we'd come in, most of Ana's attention had been on the screen, whereas I (who had seen that week's offering already, several times in at least two other theaters) had hardly glanced at it.

I turned and started back. We reached the seated workman, still looking at the movie. His short-sleeved green shirt was unbuttoned now. The peak of his cap was turned to the side. The older man knelt between the workman's knees, head moving up and down over the lap.

I sat in the empty seat beside him; and, with one hand on her hip, one hand holding her wrist, I guided Ana bodily into the chair ahead of me.

She sat, still looking at the screen.

I said softly, "Back here . . ."

Twisting to look at me, she said, "Where . . . ? What . . . ?"

Just then the workman, who, when I'd sat next to him, had made no response at all as my arm had slid down by his, suddenly blinked, pulled his hands back on the chair arms, and moved his whole body two inches forward. "That's a girl—?"

The guy sucking raised his head and craned around below the seat back.

"It's okay," I said. "Go on."

The workman looked at me. "She wanna do somethin'?" He turned to Ana. "You wanna do somethin' . . . ? If you do, that's okay!"

The man between his legs still looked back. He held the workman's dark penis in his pale fist. "Is this all right for you?" he asked Ana.

Looking down, Ana said, "Huh? Oh! Sure . . . Go on."

With (I think she found it surprising) a wink at Ana, the man on his knees went back to sucking.

The workman's hands slipped forward again on the chair arms.

Fifteen seconds later, the man sucking raised his head again. Again he held the workman. Softly he said, looking back and up at Ana, "Do you . . . want some of this?" His other hand moved to my lap, as he spoke. "I'll do your friend, if you want. And you can have this one . . ."

Ana said, "That's all right. I'm just watching."

"Oh. All *right*!" He whispered it as if reassuring her he'd keep a mutual secret. His hand slipped from my pants, and he went back to sucking.

When the workman came—"Hey, thanks. Thanks. Thank you" (one had gone to the man sucking; the other had gone to me; and the third to Ana)—he buttoned his shirt, stepped over me, patted Ana's shoulder, and was gone.

Getting up from the floor (I helped him; and Ana offered a steadying hand), the older man stopped to lay a finger on Ana's forearm. "Did that look good to you, sweetheart?"

"*Uh* . . . yes," she said, a little uncertain.

The man turned to give my arm a squeeze, then winked at me. Stepping among three other men who had stopped to watch, he whispered, "Good!" and was gone in the other direction.

Ana and I spent another hour in the theater. Once she sat on the balcony rail and watched two more guys work out in the seats beside her. For a while, on the same side of the balcony, at the end, she stood near a group of men (including one of the kids we'd passed on the stairs) and watched me trade off doing and getting done with a guy in squeaking leather, pants and jacket. Once, during a lull, as several other of the observers had been doing from time to time, she reached in to feel his erect cock—and, with his sudden frown (though he did not pull back), I and Ana both realized that, only then, had he seen she was a woman.

Ana let go and stepped quickly back, though.

Before we left, she told me, "I'm going to walk around by myself for five minutes."

When, three minutes and thirty-eight seconds later by my watch, she rejoined me at the back of the orchestra, I asked: "Everything okay?"

"Yes." She nodded.

"Anything happen?" I was quite as curious as to what she had seen as she had been to see it.

"Well, one guy made a pass at me—if you could call it a pass. In here, I mean. He asked me would I let him . . . eat me. Only, I could tell: He *really* thought I might say yes. And, when I said, 'No, thank you,' he smiled, shrugged—he did look sad—and . . . walked away."

I laughed at her surprise and we pushed through the dull gold drapes hanging across the inner door.

When we were outside I said, "So. What did you think?"

The first thing she said was, "There really *were* guys giving other guys blow jobs downstairs in the orchestra! I thought you were kidding when you first told me that. I thought it was all going to be going on in dark corners." Eyes befuddled by the full light, by the trees, and people, and the streets themselves, the garbage along the curb, the bars and clothing shops and kids and parents moving quickly about, we strolled back down Fourteenth Street, dazzled in the ordinariness of day. "It was interesting." Then she added, "It was more relaxed than I thought it was going to be. I thought it would be more frenetic—people just grabbing each other and throwing them down in the shadows and having their way. But it was so easygoing. And you didn't tell me . . ." She paused.

"Didn't tell you what?"

"—that so many people say 'no.' And that everybody pretty much goes along with it."

"I guess," I said, "when so many people say 'yes,' the 'nos' don't seem so important."

"Well, there're still *more* 'nos' than 'yesses.'"

"Between five-to-one and eight-to-one, I'd estimate."

She laughed.

"Would you go again?"

She thought. Then, with her black, curly hair, she gave a small, definite head shake. "No."

"Why not?"

"Well . . . I was scared to death!"

"Was there anything in there that scared you?"

She thought again. "No." Finally she said: "The people weren't as pretty as I thought."

Not sure what she meant, I raised an eyebrow.

"The people in the movies," she explained. "The actors on the screen. They weren't even as good-looking as the people walking around the theater."

"Oh," I said.

III

Back then—in '75 or '76—the Metropolitan and a number of the theaters in the Forty-second Street area were being fed a stream of all but amateur work. Appearing in film after film, the main actor was an avuncular guy in his late thirties. His screen persona was friendly enough and soft-spoken. Certainly he was not ugly. But he was a little dumpy, and he was distinctly bald. No one would have looked at him twice on the street.

The women in the films were equally ordinary looking and ranged in age from twenty to forty. Myself, I found almost nothing in the films themselves sexually exciting; but the sheer humanity of the figures, suddenly blown up larger than life, naked for all to see, yes, had its own interest.

The porn actors' ordinary looks that Ana had noted—both the men's and the women's—were going to change over the next three or four years. By the eighties a whole new stable of actors had taken over the city's pornography screens. They were younger. Many of them, now, were traditionally prettier. Still, a number of the men—Mark Stevens, Bobby Astyr, Jamie Gillis, the young Ron Jeremy (who would fellate himself at least once in each of his first twenty or thirty films)—were better known for their general oddness than for their looks. Even the one who was to become the best known—John Holmes—was nobody's Robert Redford.

Many of them had a fair amount of filmic charisma, such as the always-to-be-mentioned-first sexy/comic Empress of Porn, Vanessa del Rio—or the wonderfully menacing Jamie Gillis.

I want to say that, despite Ana's assertion from more than twenty years ago—"Would you go again?" "No." "Why?" "I was scared to death"—I don't see any reason that a woman (or women) couldn't take any (or every) role I've already described or will go on to describe for any (and every) male theater patron. That includes the guy joking with his cousin and his cousin's friends, coming down the stairs, genitals exposed—though it does unmitigated violence to the West's traditional concept of "women." But I believe it is only by inflicting such violences on the concept that we can prevent actual violence against women's bodies and minds in the political, material world. Though I shall not return to this topic until the close of the second essay (with Ana I have all but exhausted my firsthand material on women visiting the sex movies—though other men have told me similar tales about taking women friends with them—and, however arbitrary, that's what I have decided to restrict the material to for this first piece), I make this statement not to close off the subject but to open it up.

Besides the fear of the outside that Ana brought within, and provisional arguments about women, women in society, women in this society put aside, though the introduction of numbers of women, gay, straight, or bi, into such a scene might certainly cause some problems, those problems would nevertheless be just that: social problems to be socially solved. What waits is for enough women to consider such venues as a locus of possible pleasure. I felt that way twenty years ago. Nothing I've heard from the reports in two decades of women's bars and lesbian nights at male leather bars and the reports of men and women from heterosexual sex clubs has made me suspect I am wrong. But this is to take off into a realm of speculation that, at this point, I will table until the end of the next part of this book. I return to an account of what things I actually saw.

I never thought of the sex movie houses—the theaters that showed straight porn and encouraged gay sex in the audience—as dangerous, at least for the regular repeat attendees. Come back six times in five weeks, and you recognized a third of the faces you saw, and they recognized you. After another six visits, you had a few

On the west side of Eighth Avenue, the arched-arcade facade was, for many years, part of the Cameo Theater, an early pornographic venue. Shortly after the mid-eighties, it became the Adonis for a few years, switching screen-fare from straight to gay. The Adonis had been hounded out of its former home on Fifty-first Street and Eighth Avenue by a lawyer for World Wide Plaza, who feared the residents of the new luxury apartments would not want a gay porn theater a block to their north.

passing acquaintances, often among the particularly social queens clustering in their corner of the theater, who, now and again, singly or in pairs, would forage out to check the side seats, the balcony, the forward rows, and who were quick with their warnings:

"Honey, watch out for that guy over there. He's up to no good!"

"There've been three *very* loud arguments in the balcony in the last two hours, baby. I'd stay down here if I was you."

"Sweetheart, there's a suspicious man been hangin' around downstairs in the john since this afternoon. Frankly, *I* think he's a narc."

In the early years, if you fell asleep in the movies (as was fairly common once you shot your load, especially if you'd brought in a sixpack of beer, a hip flask of wine, or a bottle of vodka), you could wake to find your hip pants pockets slit with a razor and your change gone or your wallet empty on the seat beside you. Many times when I saw one of the slash artists sliding in beside a snoozing patron, I'd go into the row behind, reach over, and jog the sleeper's shoulder till he woke—while the razor man got up, snarled at me, and fled.

Once, in the Brandt Theater on Forty-second Street proper, just as I was coming in, a black guy in a gray fisherman-style sun hat leapt up from his seat on the aisle, planted himself in front of me, exclaimed, "*I* know who you are! You're the guy who keeps waking everybody up! Who do you think you are—the fuckin' Lone *Ranger*?" then gave me a double-fisted punch in the chest. I reeled back three steps, arms flailing, while the man turned and all but ran down the aisle—the only retribution I ever suffered for my good deeds.

In the Cameo once, I saw the following operation pulled by two black guys in their late twenties, early thirties. The victim was an older white man, maybe sixty, in a suit and tie.

As the gentleman came down the aisle, sight dim from the daylight outside, one of the assailants rose abruptly from his chair, turned, bumped into him roughly, and immediately started an argument: "Hey, man, *why'd* you bump into me? Watch where you're goin', huh? What were you, born in a *barn*? Don't you got no manners? You're a fuckin' rude asshole, you know that? What—you just bump into *everybody*, don't you? *You* don't give a fuck!" By now he was pushing the man in the chest (who was apologizing, trying to explain that, really, it was unintentional, he simply couldn't see . . .), backing him up the aisle.

Waiting at the back of the theater, now the accomplice hurried down and, just behind the older man, dropped to one knee with his fists on the floor, facing to the side.

The first man gave the older a big shove, so that he stumbled over the kneeling man, to fall back, flailing, in the aisle. Then both were on him, the kneeling man taking his pants pockets, the other quickly going inside his jacket, yanking out whatever was there. Then both were up and running with whatever they'd gotten (four hands: four pockets) to push, pell-mell after each other, out the theater.

From the older man's fall to the moment the two barreling figures blotted the sunlight through the briefly opened lobby door was no more than eight seconds. Only now did the older man, his jacket and his pants pockets ripped, a cut on his temple from the fall, a slash on his hand from where he'd grabbed at a broken theater chair arm to stop his fall, at last begin to call out: "Help me . . . ! Please . . . ! Help me! I've been robbed . . . !"

The buzz in the theater when the police arrived made it clear it had happened a few times before. Eventually the story was that one of these older victims was the wrong lawyer, public prosecutor, or upper-administration city civil servant. The theater hired security guards soon after. The police, so the queens reported, got some special urging to catch this pair and make them an example—and did. But it confirmed for me what I'd already intuited: porn theaters were not a place to enter wearing good clothes or looking as if you had something. But that was the closest thing to real violence I ever saw there—over *thousands* of visits. And though there was still the odd argument in the balcony, the odd attempt to pickpocket someone down front, by the first years of the eighties these and the razorings stopped. (*Was it because AIDS scared away all but the most committed, on all fronts?*) And the movies just seemed generally safer.

For a decade I favored the Cameo, which eventually became the New Adonis when the old Adonis was hounded out of its home on Fifty-first Street by a lawyer for World Wide Plaza, then newly under construction. Most of my activity for the past decade and a half centered on the Capri, one of three theaters on the east side of Eighth Avenue between Forty-fifth Street and Forty-sixth, across from the M.A.S.H. Army Surplus Supply Shop, a One-Hour Photo, and the Century Loan

Building, crouched between the apartment buildings either side. (The Cameo/New Adonis finally became the Playpen peep show—in pink, blue, pink neon: "Live!" "Live!" "Live!") In the seventies the Capri was Al Goldstein's Capri, owned by the publisher and editor of *Screw Magazine*, his name proudly at the top of the marquee. But Goldstein unloaded it by the time the seventies turned over into the eighties, under the first pressure of the developers to start the "renovation" of the area.

IV

I often thought about taking photographs in the movies. But I never did. Verbal accounts such as this are what remain.

Furthest down the block from the Capri, the Venus was generally a little too scroungy even for me. The drug activity there was often so high as to obliterate the sex activity. Still, on and off through the years, it provided me with a couple of memorable regulars. Gary was one, a handyman who worked at a Catholic church on Tenth Avenue. A lanky, affable guy with a brown ponytail, he impressed me as someone with very fixed habits who, as long as he was within them, was comfortable. And he always seemed comfortable in the theater. I first met him up at the Hollywood when he was about thirty-seven, but their patrolling and monitoring turned him off, so he moved down to the Venus. Regularly he brought in his two forty-two-ounce bottles of beer, generally to sit in the last three or four rows of the orchestra on the right as you came in, settling back to wait for one of three older guys to service him, me among them. He had a regular girlfriend, he claimed, who'd introduced him to the pleasures of getting things shoved up his behind when he had sex, but her overall sexual appetites simply weren't as high as his. That's why he came to the movies. He liked two or three fingers thrust deep up his asshole while you sucked his rather thick, cut seven inches, but he was a little reticent about explaining this to new guys. So he pretty much stuck to the three of us.

If two of us showed up at the same time, he would take firm and polite charge: "No, *you* stay—and I'll see you the next time, all right?" We never argued—at least I didn't, since after the first six months I became pretty much his first choice, a fact of which I was exorbitantly, if quietly, proud. When Gary came to the theater, he was there between three hours and all day. About half that time he wanted sex. The other half, he just wanted to sit and talk quietly, occasionally taking a swig from the beer bottle, which he kept down on the bare concrete between his running shoes. By and large he did not share.

I say there were three of us. Over the years, however, there must have been a few replacements, for several times I was away for as long as a school term. But my returns rarely got a larger comment than, "Hey, how're you doin'? I *thought* that was you when I saw you come in. I haven't seen you for a while." Sitting up in his seat, he'd frown through the lenses of his gold framed glasses, fiddling with the buttons of his jeans with a big knuckled hand, zipping closed his fly, which had apparently been open. "Watch my beer for me, okay? I'm gonna run downstairs and take a piss. When I come back, we can do some stuff." If you wanted to talk about where you'd been or what you'd been doing, he was intelligently interested. "But," as he said several times, "I don't pry."

Gary was not profligate with information about the other men who serviced him. But once, when I came by and an older fellow with short white hair, a blue sweater, and white jeans got up from the seat beside him and turned up the aisle to leave, he told me as I sat down in the man's place, "He's a really nice guy. I've known him for years. Really nice—a doctor. He's interesting, too. The only thing is, I can't come with him. He's okay for the first hour or so. But after that, when I'm ready to do the deed, I have to send him away and wait for you or someone else who can get me off—or do it myself."

Gary sometimes spoke of a friend with whom he had a regular eight o'clock Thursday night chess date. Sometimes, toward seven, as he got ready to leave the theater, he'd say, "Well, I'm off to play chess"—another activity he could never interest his girlfriend in. Gary was good conversation and good sex. Our before and after talks were largely about books and magazine articles. Once, when, leaving him, I happened to drop my keys on the floor, he found them five minutes later and went through some three days of considerable effort to get them—success-fully—back to me. When I saw him last, about two or three months before the theaters shut down for good, he was celebrating his forty-sixth birthday by spending the day at the porn films.

"Good God, Gary! You're forty-*six*? That means I've known you six, maybe seven years now!"

"No, professor, I think it's a little longer." He was one of only three people in the theaters who called me by that nickname.

Another regular who spent more time at the Venus than the Capri was Tommy. All but homeless, small and muscular, he collected scrap metal off the street and sold it to the yards around the docks. For most of the years I knew him Tommy wore a sleeveless denim jacket and a studded leather band on one wrist. In the winter, one or two hooded sweatshirts turned up under the denim; in summer, a T-shirt or, often, nothing. He had a carrot-colored ponytail and a red bushy beard even larger than mine. I first ran into him back in the seventies at the Cameo. In the world of quick, perfunctory sex, he was an extremely affectionate man, so that it was always a pleasure to trick with him. (I mean, with hands, arms, hips, Tommy made love to your head. Nor did he mind necking.) Sometimes his conversation was a bit incoherent (and grew more so over the years), consisting of complaints, more or less cheerfully offered, about various of his relatives, the intricate tales about whom he always assumed I would remember from the last time we'd spoken. Once, as far back as the seventies, when I brought a newspaper into the movies with me, and, as we were talking, I showed him some article or other, he turned to me under the wall light where we were sitting and said, "No, you got to read it to me." And it hit me: Tommy didn't read or write. We last had anything to do with each other perhaps a month before the theaters closed for good—that bushy red hair was more than half white. And for a three- or three-and-a-half-year period, toward the end of the eighties, in the middle of every third or fourth session with Tommy suddenly he'd urinate all over himself. "Some guys really get off on it," he told me, once. "Uncle Phil, now—Afterwards, they'll even go down to Robbins, buy me a new pair of jeans, and bring 'em back here to the movies, so I can change into something dry. Other guys, they'd get all twisted out of shape—soon as they feel my jeans get hot and start drippin', they jump up and run out of the theater! That really tickles me. I mean, I actually get off on it! But I can't do that *too* much, you know? You know my Uncle Phil? My Uncle Phil I told you about him? Not my cousin Mary. Huh? Oh—or they won't let me into the theater"—another reason Tommy preferred the laxer and funkier Venus, especially in its end days, to the Capri.

Between '84 and '90 I was without any live-in significant other. Early in that time, I remember, when I ran into Tommy in the Venus (and his tales about his bemusing relatives were a little more coherent than later), I invited him over to my house for breakfast. "See," he explained, "I gotta have breakfast about four-thirty. My aunt—yeah, my aunt. She started that with me. 'Cause if I ain't on the street and working by six, everybody else gets all the good pieces." So, yeah, he'd come over at four-thirty—and the night before I outdid myself at Zabar's, getting stuff to grace our homefried potatoes and sunnyside-up eggs: fresh fruit, smoked salmon, toasted bagels, cream cheese, some good coffee. . . .

Tommy never showed.

When I saw him again, his excuse—whatever it was—was reasonable. We set it up again. Again he didn't show. I soothed myself with the observation that a good breakfast and an early start were good for *me*, anyway—even if I had to eat alone. Indeed, all five times he stood me up turned into wonderfully productive days at the word processor. Though the last two (by now I knew enough not to make any special trips to Broadway, unless it was just for myself), I'd have been surprised if he'd arrived. If he turned up, we'd eat what I had around. And, of course, he didn't. In the theater, though, he was always pleased to see me. And the sex was always good.

A glib wisdom holds that people like this just don't want relationships. They have "problems with intimacy." But the salient fact is: These *were* relationships. In Tommy's case, in Gary's, and in several others they were relationships that lasted years. Intimacy for most of us is a condition that endures, however often repeated, for minutes or for hours. And these all had their many intimate hours. But, like all sane relationships, they also had limits.

Eventually (four or five years later) I asked Tommy why, whenever I'd invited him over, he'd blown me off.

"Huh? I don't know." Sitting there beside me in the theater, he didn't sound uncomfortable with the subject, so I pressed it. "Well," he said finally, "maybe it's Joey, my cousin. And maybe it's that when I first started comin' to the movies, a couple of guys gave me their address and told me to come over. A few times, I went—they weren't home. Or they'd given me the wrong address; the wrong phone number. Just like Mary—she'd do something like that. Did I ever tell you about my uncle? What was his name—?"

"Phil?"

"No, not him . . . Anyway. One time there wasn't even any building at the place the guy told me to show up. So I just figured talking about it, planning it, that was the fun part. The rest, though, that was all bullshit." (I wondered if, relatives aside, that's what Flaubert had had in mind in the closing chapter of *Sentimental Education*?) "I probably figured it was some kind of joke you were pullin' that I didn't understand but wished you wouldn't do it. I went along with it, you know, while we were in the theater, I guess, tryin' to be nice. But you *really* wanted some guy like *me* to come over to your house . . . ? Damn—I think you're probably just jokin' now. Naw, I wouldn't do that; go where anybody in here told me to. *Un-uhn!* I might even get hurt or somethin'."

·   ·   ·

I think of the middle eighties in the sex movies as the "Great Winnowing," from crack and AIDS—with crack very *much* the leading villain of the two. If I gather the tragedies, most of the ones I remember come from that period: '84, '85, '86 . . .

Pietro was a shy, beefy, nineteen-year-old Italian, whom I first met in the Cameo, when he was six months in the country and living with his sister in Brooklyn. Five or six times I took him from the theater for pasta at Pizza King over on Ninth Avenue. Several times I brought him down paper bags full of clothes (which he needed, desperately), and which he could just squeeze into. I would see him wearing them, over the next two, three, four weeks, sometimes in the theater, sometimes walking in the street. Not overly swift, but not particularly slow either, he was the quintessential nice, friendly, naive kid.

Hustling? The first time I met him, he didn't even *know* the word in English.

By the time he was twenty-five, however, a lot of that beef had been pared away by coke. He was in and out of the hustling bars in the neighborhood like a figure in a fast-motion slapstick sequence—Trix, Hombres, (the old) Cats (on Eighth Avenue), O'Neill's Backyard. The shyness was long gone, replaced now by an almost belligerent friendliness, necessary if you're to be any sort of successful insurance man—or hustler. A year or two later, I recall a conversation at the bar: "Hey, do you ever see Pete—that short-haired, blond Italian kid with the accent?"

"Oh, man—that kid's dead. You didn't hear about that? It was about four months ago . . ."

There was Kevin, twenty-one and dark, dark black, who, when I first met him (also in the Cameo) wore striped engineer's overalls and a train engineer's cap. His big hands, his full mouth, and his general masculine gentleness (Kevin lifted weights years before the buffed and pumped-up nineties) made him an exemplar of male beauty that still, in memory, remains powerful for me. Like Pietro, he was another regular in from Brooklyn. On the third time we made it, he told me, "I won't go with just anyone. Only special people—like you. Because you're nice." He wanted to be a musician, though I was unclear what instruments, if any, he played.

By 1985 though, this teak-colored, muscle-bound little powerhouse (he wasn't much taller than Tommy) was scooting all around the Port Authority, doing dope deals up at Gate 335, passing bags back in the underpass across from Hombres ("'Cause the police are just through the aluminum doors twenty feet away—and that's the *last* place they think you be doin' it!"). When he would run into me in the theater now, it was, "Lemme hold two dollars, man, so I can run down to the bathroom and get somethin'. Then I'll be back!" and he would—about every three minutes, with the identical plea, as many times as you'd supply the two bucks.

In '88 or '89, the last time I saw him, I was on my way to the Habana-San Juan Dry Cleaners, recently moved around the corner across from the post office on Eighty-third Street. Really, it was like the heaviest-handed Concluding Moral Resolution from some Dreiser or Dos Passos novel. Kevin was coming along, picking through the garbage cans . . .

The power was gone. The gentleness was still there, though. After our wistful three minutes of conversation (he was homeless, he was dirty and ragged, he wasn't doing too good, but . . . well, maybe things would get better), he shambled off with it to somewhere . . . I haven't seen him since.

Why *this* one should be sadder than the others, I'm not sure. But it strikes me that way. When, after a near-dozen-year reign as the largest and most successful of the West Side hustling bars, the Haymarket closed in '81, Joey (mother Polish, father Irish and Italian) was twenty-four and a two-hundred/three-hundred-dollar-a-night hustling success, with more drugs and watches and diamond rings and coke than he knew what to do with. There was a whole lot of talk about revamping Times Square—tearing everything down on Forty-second Street, building these big office towers in place of the theaters. And the whole neighborhood was shutting down and being bought up by land speculators. The high-class hustling business was all heading over to the East Side, where Rounds would shortly begin its legendary reign on Lexington Avenue. But some grow more dependent than others on familiar institutions. Joey had worked out of the Haymarket since he was seventeen and there with false I.D. His clients were all West Siders. His drug connections were all West Siders. The Haymarket had made him the success he was. Besides, his mother lived on the East Side, and he wanted to stay away from her. So while the business moved east, he remained. He had friends he could crash with—now on this couch, now on that—when it got rough. He'd always been a good guy. So, a few times he'd paid for his crash space with sex. ("They say the first time you do that, you ain't a hustler no more. You're just a faggot. Well, who the hell wants to be a hustler *all* his life?")

In preparation for the longer and longer delayed architectural renovation, the drugstore shut, the comic book shop moved, the dry cleaners closed—and two years later saw Joey living on the street. But he was still a good-looking guy, an enthusiastic raconteur, with hands as big as Kevin's (although, unlike Kevin, Joey was *not* a nailbiter), dark hair, pleasant smile—but with enough sense not to dwell too much on the glory days now two, now three, now four years in the past. When I first saw him one evening as I was walking with a friend past Trix, he was standing in front of the bar talking to some other hustlers, one hand deep in the hip pocket of his jeans, playing with himself while he joked and chatted.

Playing with his dick in his pants was what he was doing when I saw him a day later, standing alone by the doorway just down from the firehouse—and I started a conversation: "Do you always stand around pulling on yourself like that?" I asked, thinking I was being daring (breaking a level, as therapist/client-speak would have put it in those days).

"Oh, yeah. Sure. Most of the time, I don't even realize I'm doin' it. When I used to hustle, man, that's what *all* my johns would start talking to me about. But it feels good—I like to do it. It keeps me relaxed. And it's always makin' me new friends. So why should I stop? You remember the Haymarket, man? It was right there. See? The front's all cinderblocked closed now . . ."

Joey's nickname was Joey-Who-Needs-a-Bath, to distinguish him from several other guys named Joey, then out on the streets. (He could talk about drugs with guys who worked out of Trix, but the bar wouldn't let him in. He was too dirty.) He'd gotten the name in the first year after the Haymarket shut, when his requests for crash space were usually couched, "Can I come up? Man, I really need to take me a bath!" which, because most people used showers, sounded a bit quaint. "But that's what my mom always said when I was a kid. She meant shower, but since it was in a bathtub, she *said* bath. And I said it, too. It's just like *you* always say 'icebox' instead of refrigerator. I bet people laugh at you for that, too. But it probably just means you had a real icebox when you were a kid."

"That's right. And yeah, they do," I told him, "sometimes."

By now, though, in the two years he'd been on the streets, the requests for baths/showers were no longer part of his "self-presentation." Joey-Who-Needs-a-Bath was just a grubby guy, always fiddling with his dick down in his pocket.

For about a month and a half in '84 or '85, Joey and I had a regular Thursday morning meeting at ten-thirty, when we would go into the Capri together, at the end of which I would give him ten dollars, and he would run off to get some crack.

And I learned why he had been such a successful hustler. "I know guys are always telling you this, and you think it's a load of bullshit. But I'm really straight. I mean, I can get off with guys—any way till Sunday. But to do it I always have to *think* about girls. That's why I like goin' in the movies, so that I can get some good heterosexual stimulation from the screen." Though I think a certain reticence is appropriate when discussing it, at least *one* reason Pietro and Kevin were memorable is that both, uncut, were hung (in a simile) like mules. Joey was not. On a scale of small, medium, and large I fall directly on the border line between the latter two. Joey was just under the middle of medium. But, sitting beside me in the Capri, talking, with his cut dick out, he explained, "I *love* to come, man. I mean I love to come more than anything in the *world*. And I like people to *see* me come. I like them to *know* I'm coming. I like them to *hear* me come. I like them to love it that I'm coming, too! Now: You want to suck me? You want me just to jerk off? Or what?"

Between the time I'd first talked to him and now, Joey had developed a sore on the back of his left hand that was probably infected and was suppurating through its bandage. So I said: "Why don't you jerk off?"

"Sure. That's easy." Over the next twenty-five minutes, now losing his pants, now his shirt, now his shoes, next his socks, now standing and growling, now sitting all but in my lap, thrashing and flailing his free arm, now practically down between the seat and the back in front of him on the floor, he groaned and quivered and pumped till, lying back in the chair, ass up off the cushion, grinning and panting, he sprayed across his quivering stomach and began to rub his mucus around and over himself. "Oh, man . . . ! Oh, shit . . . ! Oh, fuck . . . !"

Three of the five people who had gathered in the aisle to watch, applauded.

When, finally, Joey began to sit up, collect his clothes, and put them back on, he asked, "Anybody want to contribute five bucks? I mean, you gotta admit, that was a good show, huh?"

One older gentleman gave it to him. "Thanks, pops." It went into his jeans pocket with the ten from me.

There are as many different styles, intensities, and timbres to sex as there are people. The variety of nuance and attitude blends into the variety of techniques and actions employed, which finally segues, as seamlessly, into the variety of sexual objects the range of humankind desires. Certainly one of the necessary places where socializing and sexualizing actually touch for, dare I call it, health or just contentment: We do a little better when we sexualize our own manner of having sex—learn to find our own way of having sex sexy. Call it a healthy narcissism, if you like. This alone allows us to relax with our own sexuality. Paradoxically, this also allows us to vary it and accommodate it, as far as we wish, to other people. I don't see how this can be accomplished without a statistically significant variety of partners and a fair amount of communication with them, at that, about what their sexual reactions to us are. (However supportive, the response of a single partner just cannot do that. This is a quintessentially *social* process, involving a social response.) When Lacan says, "One desires the desire of the other," self-confidence is, generally speaking, the aspect of it desired. That sexual self-confidence (though it's not what's usually meant by the words) is what Joey had; and it was very attractive.

I was the one, though, who, after a month or so, missed our assigned Thursday meeting. Hustlers are just not my particular thing. (Somebody could probably expand that into a five-hundred-page psychoanalytic study as to why. But while I've liked any number of hustlers as people, it's down among my secondary or even tertiary preferred forms of sex.) When I ran into Joey on the street, he was all professional concern: "I was worried about you, man. I mean, I was hoping that nothing had happened to you or anything. The money I could always get from *somebody*."

I made my excuses—then, responsibly, suggested we put off our next meeting. (One of the good things about hustlers is that usually they tend not to take such things personally.) And we were just passing friends north of the Deuce.

Oh, we had a couple more encounters. The last, most pleasant, messiest (on my part) and loudest (on his) was in a doorway on Forty-eighth Street, one night when I'd had a couple too many. Afterwards Joey put me on an uptown bus, then tramped off over the icy street into the December dark. It was only five bucks that night.

In '86 or '87 one February evening at (the Eighth Avenue) Cats, a black drag queen with exquisite crimson nails and a red-blond wig frowned at me over her drink, then asked, "Are you Chip?"

"That's right."

"Did you know a kid out here named Joey? They used to call him Joey-Who-Needs-a-Bath?"

"Sure."

"He used to talk about you, a lot. I thought, because of the beard—and the glasses—you might be him. You know he died two weeks back."

I turned around. "No, I *didn't!*"

She nodded. "They found him in a lobby behind the stairs in a building on Forty-eighth—frozen to death. They think he had a heart attack or something. Oh, that boy was *just* the sweetest! I used to let him stay with me all the time. On my couch. He was always so nice." Now she leaned over and put her hand on my wrist. "I have never known anyone who could get into sex more than he could. I mean, that boy *loved* to come!"

"Yes, I know."

"I mean—" a bit loaded, she was just on the other side of discretion—"I have a few little kinks, myself, and he was always the world's most obliging lay. You see, I like to get fucked in unusual places. Once, when he came by looking for a place to stay, I threw him into the shower, dried him off, stuck him in an old suit jacket of mine from the last time I had a straight job—it just about fit him—and took him to the Rainbow Room. You ever been to the Rainbow Room, honey?"

"On the top of Rockefeller Center? Yes . . ."

"And I made him fuck me in the stall in the ladies' room." She sat back now. "And that boy was *not* quiet when he came. Another time—" she turned and pointed toward the door—"right across the street there in Beefsteak Charlie's. You ever been in there? They got the back room, which is three steps down from the front, and off around the side. They close that at nine-thirty, before they kick everybody out at ten. Well, honey, we went right in there—and he did me out on one of the tables. I mean, half the waiters was in there, eggin' us on. I don't know what the manager thought—if he knew. And don't *tell* me about the Staten Island

Ferry at midnight—" She shook her head. "That boy was *so* talented. I don't think he'd had his twenty-ninth birthday yet." She shook her head once more. "Frozen to death in a hallway—with a heart attack. I think the drugs must have weakened his system."

The period had its AIDS tragedies ("You remember your little hustler friend Mark?" a redheaded hustler, Tony, in black leather pants and black leather jacket, who specialized in heavy S&M topping, told me one evening, elbow to elbow with me at the bar in Trix. "Two weeks before he died, we all got together and sent him home—upstate, to Binghamton. He wanted to die at home. So we sent him there. And he did.") and jailhouse cases (blue-eyed, black-haired Paul, who came out of Rikers Island correctional facilities, back to the Venus, with the worst case of crabs I've *ever* seen; and hulking German John, whom I met on the strip when he was twenty-one [with his own movie tales: "Once this guy takes me into the Cameo, and he has me take my sneakers off and sit in the row behind him and put my feet over the seats in front. Then he plays with them, and kisses them, and fondles 'em and stuff—and they were pretty damned powerful, too, 'cause I'd been sleeping on the street for almost three weeks by then"] and who, eighteen years later, *still* writes and phones me now and again from jail in Southern California, where he's been serving time for the last six years. And scruffy little "Sundance" McLoughlin, missing a forefinger from a motorcycle accident, a regular in the back balcony of the Capri, who last phoned me from jail in Toronto).

But not all tales end in premature death or incarceration. For most, indeed, we never learn an end at all.

Maybe thirty-six, Bobby lived in Oliver Sacks land. Homeless, he collected cans and frequented the Capri for about three years in the late eighties. Among our dozen encounters in the theater, I took him home with me some three times. Once, in the midst of sex, suddenly he insisted that I "fuck him like a whore!" Bobby didn't know where he was from, what his last name was—and was unclear on his first. ("Bobby" was just the one I picked for him; but, in his vague, friendly way, he responded pretty much to any name you addressed him by.) The last time I saw him, sometime in '87 or '88, sitting on the island in the middle of Broadway, with his green plastic garbage bag of empty beer and soda cans against his knee, without shoes and wearing a pair of dress pants so tight he could not close the zipper, Bobby—like the soldier of Arete—avowed with as much sincerity as he had the second, the fourth, the sixth time we'd met, and, indeed, all three times he'd come to my house, that he had no memory of me whatsoever.

There was Al, a chain-smoking, six-foot, 180-pound Italian welder from Brooklyn, in his late thirties, with a classic micro-penis: three-quarters of an inch in diameter and not quite an inch long, when erect. "And *this* didn't pop out till I was about fifteen, sixteen, and got all this damned hair—when my damned balls finally came down." From the sleeves and collar of his blue work shirt, his arms and neck were a veritable rug, his jaw a steel-stubbled sheet in the screen's flicker. (Al's testicles were normal/small—and hairy. Both were there, though they'd descended, he explained, late in his adolescence, three months apart.) "You know, they were gonna turn me into a *girl* when I was born—the doctors? But my mom said, 'No fuckin' *way!*' Thank God I had some skin, or nobody would've known *what* I was!" Al's masturbatory technique was to sit in the first row, legs out, pants open, and flick the side of his thick thumb back and forth over his diminutive knob. "When I first come in here, it was just for the damned movies. I didn't even realize the kind of shit that went on here till I'd been comin' in for a couple of weeks. And, I mean, a lot of the guys who make out here got those fuckin' horse cocks, anyway—you see 'em sittin' around beatin' off when you walk in. Hey, did you see that black guy in here yesterday, sitting right over there, down from me in the first row? I swear, he shot all over the damned *screen*—really, he hit the movie screen! Look, it's still up there—see? I don't even think people can *piss* that far! But don't you know, I got me a regular little fan club in here. There must be about six or seven guys come in, they just think I'm the hottest thing since sliced bread. About two hours back, I had me three of 'em in here *fightin'* over me, man!" Chuckling, Al lit another cigarette, then reached down to brush ashes from his pubic hair. They'd fallen there from his last cigarette.

And there was Arly, who'd lost a leg at five when his crazed, drunken father had flung him under an oncoming subway ("You know, sometimes I still dream about them subway cars rushing over my head, man!") and who played the drums in his mother's Columbian Pentecostal church. I met him when he was twenty-one or twenty-two and he would come in to settle in the Cameo's balcony. Good-looking, friendly, and extremely agile on his one-stick crutch, for the first three times I talked to him, he claimed to be too tired for sex. Finally I'd assumed he just wasn't available, when, the next time he passed me in the balcony aisle, suddenly he seized my arm to explain in a low, excited voice (like someone taking a breath before plunging under water to perform some intricate task), that he was more highly sexed than most men, and thus anyone who sat with him but stayed only through the first of his orgasms would (in his words) "drive me crazy, man. It makes me wanna *die*—" he dragged down my arm at the emphasis—"if I can't come three or four times, you know? I mean, I wanna die. So if you wanna do me, man, you got to promise to stay with me till I come at *least* three times, huh? All right? Okay?" And so we began a regular relationship in which, well . . . *that's* what he did. Those first three orgasms usually took him about forty-five minutes. In a more relaxed, two- or two-and-a-half-hour session, he'd make five, and often six. "*Now* I'm relaxed, man. Maybe I'll get off again, or, if I go home, man, I won't feel like I wanna die, see?"

Arly's and my friendship *did* get to the point of going to each other's houses. When I first visited him, he lived in an incredibly filthy apartment in an incongruous squatters' building on West End Avenue at Ninety-eighth Street, his floor strewn inches deep with girly magazines around his corner mattress. Two years later, he moved back into his mother's neat, green-and-yellow-and-pink-and-purple-and-orange-and-blue frilly project apartment, with poodle and flamingo mirrors and colorful religious statues. A couple of times Arly came to my five-flight walk-up writer's digs. With his one leg and single-stem homemade crutch, he took my steps three at a bound.

"Arly, how do you *do* that?"

"See, I don't *weigh* as much as you guys do, by thirty, thirty-five pounds! I can go a lot faster. Besides, I live on the eighth floor, man—our elevators *never* work. So I get a lot of practice."

In '86 I remember running into him one afternoon at the Capri.

Arly was sitting under a light, crutch against the wall and sports jacket folded over the seat in front of him (after several years of panhandling on the corner of Forty-seventh Street, in the diamond sellers' neighborhood, one of the shop owners, after talking with him, had taken him in and given him a job), his pants open, jerking off. Now, at thirty, Arly was good-looking, with a hard body, and a solid ten inches, uncut; and while a few people were put off by the missing leg, he seldom lacked for takers. He demanded endurance. But he was attractive enough—and big enough—that he could afford to be choosy. As I slid in beside him, he grinned up at me and grabbed my arm to pull me down: "Aw, this is good, now—I got the man here who *really* knows how to do it!" You'd have to be a habitué to understand just how fine a greeting like that can make you feel. Arly leaned closer. "Hey, you know: I almost got me in trouble, earlier."

"What happened?" I asked, sitting—and settling my hand between his legs, moving into his open fly to rub the irregular flesh of his stump, while it flexed and shifted in response. He enjoyed that. I did too.

"I'm here this morning at ten o'clock, and I want to get off a couple of times by myself, you know, so I can relax. This guy is sitting right there in front of me— I'm not payin' him no mind. I mean, I don't even see him. And I get to work. Well, *you* know how I shoot! And I ain't done it for a couple of days. Man, it goes over the seat back there, gets all on his neck, in his hair . . . ! The next thing you know, he's up in his seat and wants to have a fight! I say, hey, hey, hey, hey, hey—man, look! I'm a cripple! You don't wanna fight me! Look at me! See? I only got one leg!"

But I'm holding my crutch—you know, I made it myself. It's metal. It can do some damage, if it has to. Guys are always hassling cripples."

"Did anything *happen*?" I asked, suitably surprised.

"Naw. He backed down. I told him I was sorry. He's a lot of mouth, though. Anyway. Finally, he got up and stomped off. It was an accident." Arly was obviously tickled by the whole thing. "But I swear. I didn't do it on purpose. I just didn't see him, you know?" His hand went up to the back of my head to urge me down.

In July of 1987, at a pre-theater dinner in Greenwich Village with two of her oldest friends, on her way to the lady's room at Gavin's restaurant, my mother suffered a massive stroke that kept her at St. Luke's Hospital for ten months, then put her in the Park Shore Manor nursing home, paralyzed on her right side and unable to speak, write anything other than incoherent progressions of letters, or respond directly to verbal instructions. In this state, wheelchair-bound and incontinent, she remained for the final eight years of her life.

The incident, as do such medical catastrophes—with hospital visits, medical consultations, visits with lawyers in a cluttered upstairs Harlem office, conservatorship papers, trips down with lawyer and doctor to the city courthouse for competency hearings in the courtroom off the echoing second-floor rotunda, and, yes, the resultant emotional strain—simply excised, as with a pair of sheers, a productive ten months from my sister's life and mine.

I am convinced that, in Kafka's *Die Verwandlung*, Gregor Samsa's transformation stands for just such a catastrophe, fallen on one or another family member: a stroke, a crippling accident, insanity (possibly Kafka's own tuberculosis), an irrevocable change that does not (immediately) kill but leaves, rather, an incomprehensible creature to be dealt with one way or another by all who remain, a creature wholly alien yet somehow recognizable in fifty little ways—a hand gesture, a shake of the head, a sudden single phrase ("I know") muttered thirty-seven times, a smile, a moue—as the subject he or she once was.

A week after my mother's transfer to the Park Shore Manor—a six-block walk beyond the last stop on the L train at the far end of Canarsie—on my way home from my second visit, I dropped in to the Capri.

And found Arly.

He'd come three times already (he explained), so, after forty-five minutes (in which he came three more), we fell into conversation, and I began to tell him some of the trials of the previous year. When I told him about the visit to the nursing home, he declared, "Hey, why don't I come out and see your mom with you? When's the next time you're goin'?"

I said, "Huh?"

"No, I'm serious. I'll go out with you, next time you have to go—and visit with your mother. It'll be better for you, if you got company on that long subway ride, won't it?"

". . . Huh?"

He punched me in the shoulder—playfully. "I'm not kiddin'. I'd really like that. When you goin' again?"

"Huh . . . ?" I repeated. "You want to come with me—all the way to *Canarsie?*"

"Sure. I *love* that stuff, man. Goin' to visit people in the hospital, in nursing homes. That's fun. I told you—my mother had this church? That's what we used to do all the time when I was a kid. Go around and visit sick people. Man, that was the most fun I ever had in my *life!* They were real interesting, those people. Old people—they could tell some stories—"

"My mom doesn't talk any more," I said.

"That's okay. It's still fun. When you gonna go again?"

"*Uhh* . . . ," I said. "In two weeks. On Thursday. My sister goes every week. I've been trying to go every other week."

"Good," he said. "You just tell me where you wanna meet."

So, two Thursdays hence, we met at my stoop and rode down to Fourteenth, transferred to the lonely L, and took the train to the end of the line to get out on the bustling Brooklyn avenue. On his single crutch, Arly lurched along beside me through the June sun to the Park Shore.

In my mom's room on the seventh floor, Arly became a one-legged whirlwind, straightening her pillow, putting things right on the table beside her bed—the crutch was left in the corner now: in such small spaces he found it easier to maneuver without it—telling her how well she looked, smoothing up her covers, reassuring her that she'd soon be well. Mom's sluggishness over the first fifteen minutes of our visit gave way to a bright-eyed attention, as if by osmosis she absorbed his energy and his cheerfulness. Clearly she was enchanted with him, and grinned and nodded and followed him with her eyes. Several times she even laughed. We took her downstairs in her wheelchair and outside on a forty-minute tour of the neighborhood, stopping for ice cream, which, back in the grassy yard in the back of the Manor on our return, first I, then Arly fed her with a white plastic spoon.

"She likes music," I said. "Can you sing?"

"Naw," Arly said. "I play the drums, but I don't sing too good—" then sang with me anyway: "She'll Be Comin' Round the Mountain," "When the Saints Go Marchin' In," and "Jesus Loves Me," Arly in Spanish, me in English, as, in her orange robe in the wheelchair, her paralyzed arm belted with white Velcro into its fiberglass brace, Mom "la-la-ed" along.

If you're looking for an analogue from literature, it's not Gregor's sister playing the violin outside her transformed brother's door; it's the young peasant who tells the meaningless jokes as he lets Ivan rest his feet on his shoulders, the only position in which the dying man can be comfortable, in *The Death of Ivan Ilyich*.

Over the years Arly'd mentioned both coke and crack. But now, in the late eighties, when I ran into him in the theater he usually had a hip bottle of Dewars with him. A couple of times, holding it up and looking at it in the light from the theater's wall lamp, he told me, "Man, scotch is what saved me from being a crackhead!"

And once, already tipsy, he came ringing my doorbell with a quart bottle already half empty. While we were sitting on my maroon living room rug, talking about one thing and another, suddenly he reached out, pulled me to him, and, with his eyes closed, kissed me for ten or fifteen uninterrupted minutes—which he'd certainly never done before in the theater!

When we broke, he said, "Now—I ain't never done *that* before! I mean with a guy. *That* was interesting. First I was trying to pretend like your beard was pussy hair or something. But I didn't even really have to do *that*!"

Good stuff, that Dewars.

In 1984 I'd written a novel with a character based on Arly, about whom I'd tried to imagine what it would be like running into after a decade's absence. The reality was less dramatic, more unusual, and probably—for some—more predictable.

In the summer of '93, when I was sitting out on my stoop reading, around the corner came a rotund fellow on a crutch, with natty tan slacks carefully pinned up on his missing leg, a single polished loafer (I seem to remember that he wore no sock; but possibly the one he wore was the same coffee-and-cream tan as his skin), hair thinning on the top, and his arm around an extraordinarily attractive and fresh-looking black-haired woman. Arly must have been forty, even forty-two by then. No, it hadn't been ten years since I'd seen him, but it *had* been at least three.

"Hey, man. I was *wondering* if I was going to run into you today. This is my wife, man—isn't she beautiful?" (The woman couldn't have been more than twenty-two or twenty-three.) "We been married about six months now—well, she ain't *really* my wife. But we been livin' together—in my mother's apartment. For six months. My mom, she went back to Colombia, so I got the apartment now. She don't speak no English, but she *loves* to take care of me—" he gave me a quick wink—"almost as good as you used to. Isn't she beautiful, man? She's just twenty years old. Isn't she the most beautiful woman in the *world*?"

I'll tell you, you could make a case for it.

With her arm around Arly's shoulder, her bright dark eyes, her white blouse and printed peasant skirt, she looked like a girl in love.

"And she *cooks* . . . ? Man, can she cook!" Arly patted his stomach, of which there were thirty or so pounds more since I'd last seen him. "She got me lookin' like a house. But she loves me like this. She knows all about me, everything I need, how to take care of me."

"So I guess you don't go to the movies any more?"

"Oh, no, man. I don't need that shit now. That place is nasty. I don't like to go there no more. Yeah, I still got me a few videos. But she even lets me watch *them*, you know? She watches 'em with me. She's perfect, man! I mean, isn't she *perfect*?" He pulled her nearer. "You guys gonna have to come up to our place for dinner. How about that, you hear?"

My significant other had just walked up to the stoop: I introduced Dennis to Arly and to the perfect young woman whose name we hadn't been told.

"Yeah, you guys come on up. I'll call you—I still got your number. You'll come on up for dinner. I mean, you wanna taste some *real* good food, the way she cooks . . . ? You gotta come up—for dinner."

"Thanks, Arly. Sure."

With her shoulder under his arm, Arly turned and, on his crutch, made his way with her back to the corner.

I haven't seen them since.

Despite moments of infatuation on both sides, these were not love relationships. The few hustlers excepted, they were not business relationships. They were encounters whose most important aspect was that mutual pleasure was exchanged—an aspect that, yes, colored all their other aspects, but that did not involve any sort of life commitment. Most were affable but brief because, beyond pleasure, these were people you had little in common with. Yet what greater field and force than pleasure can human beings share? More than half were single encounters. But some lasted over weeks; others for months; still others went on a couple of years. And enough endured a decade or more to give them their own flavor, form, and characteristic aspects. You learned something about these people (though not necessarily their name, or where they lived, or what their job or income was); and they learned something about you. The relationships were not (necessarily) consecutive. They braided. They interwove. They were simultaneous. (Several times I saw Gary in the morning and Arly and/or Tommy in the afternoon.) These relationships did not annoy or in any way distress the man I was living with—*because* they had their limits. They were not the central relationships of my life. They made that central relationship richer, however, by relieving it of many anxieties.

V

Mulling back over it, generally the denizens of the Venus seemed a bit more colorful than those from the Capri: the extremely handsome Hispanic young man who would rush into the theater at ten after five, obviously just off from work, drop down in the first row, pull out his genitals and a *serious* looking pair of handcuffs, bind his scrotum up in them, their hasp ratcheting through the catch, masturbate, and then, putting himself and the whole metallic contraption back in his pants, rush from the theater equally fast (as far as I could tell, he must have kept the key at home); or the various fellows—those who did not lean suddenly forward to spill on the back of the chair before them or on the cement floor in front of the cracked red seat—who, a moment after coming, would fall asleep, pants still gaping, genitals still loose, semen glimmering on their brown or black bellies in the light from the screen; the several midgets; the countless drag queens; the dozen who, off in the darkest parts of the theater, would strip completely naked before masturbating. . . .

Between the Venus and the Capri was the Eros I: Unlike the Venus and the Capri, the Eros showed gay porn films. After performing on stage, male dancers came out to walk the aisles and hustle the audience ("You want a private show—thirty-five dollars, downstairs?")—but for me the whole thing was too mercenary, too formalized, and—like hustlers—go-go dancers in general aren't my thing.

This essay's purpose is to present a vernacular periplum of what might be found in the Times Square gay cruising venues and the culture that grew up around them, as well as to suggest an overview of what went on in Manhattan straight pornographic theaters encouraging gay sex over those years. I believe I've done that, and done it honestly. But it would be untrue to leave you with the sense that I never saw any psychologically troubling events.

A homeless man at least in his late seventies, possibly in his eighties, slept in a right-hand seat of the Venus's balcony. I saw him *every* time I went into the theater, over more than a five-year period. Finally I realized, quite outside any of the sex or drugs, he lived there—permanently. He left the theater only for the few hours during the night it closed for cleaning. He was there three days before the door of the Venus was boarded over and chained. Three weeks later I saw him in his tweed cap and ragged jacket, wandering along the street, eyes squinting in his wrinkled face, as though the wan Eighth Avenue sun was simply and permanently too bright.

The west side of the block between Forty-fifth and Forty-sixth Streets held three small theaters. Toward the north end stood the Capri, with a narrow orchestra (six seats on the left of the aisle, three seats to the right) and a narrower balcony. The bus stopped directly before it so that waiting passengers often used its small triangular marquee during the rain. After a small parking lot just to the Capri's south stood the Eros I with orchestra and downstairs dressing rooms. (In the 1970s, there was an Eros II, but that closed years ago.) Then came the Venus. With the smallest entrance of these three theaters, the Venus was the largest—and the most rundown: eight seats to the left of the aisle running down through the orchestra and six to the right. The balcony had a three-row front section, separated by an aisle and an iron railing from an eight-row rear section, with an aisle up the middle. From the 1980s on, all three theaters switched from 35-millimeter film to video projection. The Capri and the Venus showed straight pornography. The Eros I alternated gay videos with live male dancers.

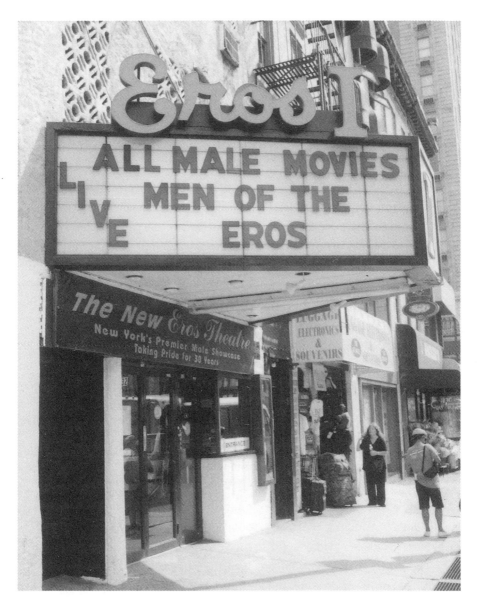

Once, on a November weekday morning three years ago, as I came into the Capri and sat down in the orchestra, I noticed a bushy-headed fellow a few rows ahead. His fresh, open profile was lit by one of the theater wall lights directly over him. Only after a few moments did I see that he wore two beat-up winter coats, one over the other, suggesting he was homeless. When I had been there about ten minutes, suddenly he stood up, shrugged off one coat, then the other—beneath them he wore a limp T-shirt with a couple of holes—unbuckled the belt of his tan pants, and let them drop (he wore no underpants), showing his bony buttocks.

After standing like that a few moments, he bent over, eyes still on the screen, pulled his pants up, buckled them, then sat again for another eight, nine, ten minutes. Then, again, he stood up in his T-shirt and slacks—the pants were very dirty—and this time bent to disappear below the chair backs. Oh, I thought, he's a crackhead, forever searching the floor for someone else's dropped bits of the drug.

He stayed down a full minute, doing whatever he was doing on the floor. Then, like a large dust mop, his curly head rose above the chipped orange rims and again he sat in the seat to watch the film.

He stayed put another fifteen minutes. When I was seconds away from getting up to go prowl the theater on my own, again he stood. Now he climbed up on his chair seat, pulled loose his T-shirt, stripped it over his head, and tossed it down. Once more he unbuckled his pants and dropped them to his feet.

Standing in his chair, against the video projection with, at the edge of the screen, its green and pink striations, the scrawny youngster with the bushy head—naked now—watched the film another full minute.

Around us, three or four people laughed.

More or less jovially, a black voice called from the theater's back row: "Hey, you fuckin' crazy lunatic, sit *down*!"

More people laughed.

The young man's eyes remained on the screen, however. Only after another fifteen or twenty seconds did he slowly bend down, pull up his pants, and climb from his seat. Finding his T-shirt, once more he pulled it on over his head and sat.

Odd behavior has always intrigued me. I got up, left my row, walked three down, and moved into his. As I sat on the orange theater seat, three away from him, he stood up again, turned and lifted his seat and the seat next to his, got on his knees, and lay down on the dirty cement. As I looked at him—his head was toward my blue running shoe—he glanced up. "I'm sorry," he said softly, from the ground. "But I'm acting funny today. It don't bother you, does it . . . ?"

"No," I said. "No . . . not at all. But I was just wondering, are you all right?"

He closed his eyes to lie there another half minute. I thought my question unheard or ignored. Suddenly he began to push himself up and returned to sit, now a seat away from me. "Naw, I'm okay. I just have to do weird stuff every once in a while. It doesn't mean nothin'." The accent was working-class Jewish. So was his friendly, open face.

For another ten minutes he sat quietly, only once turning to pick up his coats, one of which had fallen to the floor, and fold them on the seat beside him.

Then, suddenly, he stood up, glanced at me with a grin, and said, "Sorry . . ." A moment later he had stripped out of his T-shirt and again dropped his pants. Standing naked, down within his fallen trousers he toed off one of his shoes, pulled one bare foot free (he wore no socks), then toed off the other. More or less keeping his eyes on the screen, he turned a full 360 degrees on his clothing pile. Above his groin to the right was an appendectomy scar. On his vaguely sunken chest, among sparse hair, was a faint splatter of acne—as there was on his cheek. Naked, he stepped over, started to sit in the chair beside me, then turned his back to me. "Look at my ass," he said. "Go on. That's good."

As twenty-year-old buttocks go, they were pretty ordinary. With a sigh he sat beside me, reached out with one foot, and pulled his pants along the floor. Leaning down to pick them up, he shook them out and started to pull them on. As he moved forward enough to pull them up under his backside, he asked me, "You don't think I'm *completely* bug-fuck crazy, do you?"

"You're pretty close," I said.

He thought that was funny and laughed. "Yeah, maybe I am, pretty much. But I don't think, really . . . I was in the hospital up in Connecticut until two days ago. But they kicked me out. I had some medicine. But I don't really like to take it." He shrugged. "Someone stole it from me anyway. I mean, it isn't even gonna get them high. It isn't that kind of dope. But some people just gotta steal anything they can get their hands on, just 'cause it belongs to someone else. But now it means I gotta walk around acting like a nut case." He pulled his pants together. "I don't know why I keep buckling them. I'm just gonna have to take them off again." Leaving the flies open, he leaned over, tugged his T-shirt from among his coats, and put it back on. Yellowed cloth slid over his armpit's dark tuft. As his head pushed through the neck, he looked at me. "You gonna help me out?" I thought he meant loose change or a couple of dollars, and readied my excuse. But he went on: "If I keep my shoes off—" he moved his thin feet over the cement—"and now and then you just look at my ass, I'll be pretty much okay. I mean, if you don't mind . . . ?"

Bemused, I asked, "Why do you keep taking your clothes off?"

"Oh," he said. "For the stimulation. So I don't . . . you know, go to sleep." He took another breath. "Or disappear. Or just . . . drift away—completely. That's why I gotta take my clothes off."

I tried not to sound confused. "What happens if you don't?"

"I told you, I just drift away. I fall asleep, maybe even stop breathing . . . and die. I'll just turn into some smoke, and then I won't be here any more. It's come close to happening, a few times, now." He looked at me. "I don't mean *really*. But my heart slows down, way down; I stop breathing—and I'll die. So I have to do weird shit—take off my clothes. Lie down in the middle of the sidewalk." He chuckled. "Sometimes I just walk into Micky-Dee's or a pizza place and I go over to somebody, drop my pants, and show 'em my ass. That's shocking, right?"

"*Um* . . . ," I said. "A little bit—sure."

"It doesn't have to be a whole lot. It's better when it's just a little bit. You can even laugh—that's okay. It's better when they laugh than when they get all upset and crazy about it. But you feel the shock—and this energy goes out from you. And I get the energy. It keeps me awake. It holds me together, so I don't just drift away and disappear—or stop breathing."

Suddenly he stood up, turned as though he were about to leave—only, once more, he dropped his pants below his buttocks.

Though he'd just described it, it *was* startling.

I did laugh. He pulled them up, turned back around and sat again. "See? And I got your energy. I'll be okay for another fifteen or twenty minutes now. You don't mind, do you?"

"I guess not," I said. "No." Then I asked, "What about sex?"

"Huh?" He looked up at me, frowning. "What? You mean you wanna fuck my ass? You're gay? My fuckin' luck—I pick some gay guy! Well, you see, *I'm* not gay. I just need the energy. And that's the best kind—when you show people your cock or your ass. Your ass is usually better. I think that's because the way the energy comes back in through the muscles there. The ass muscles are bigger—but I'm not really sure about that. Hey, you don't mind, do you?"

I laughed now. "Yes, I *am* gay. But what I had in mind was giving you a blow job—sucking your dick. I thought maybe something like that might relax you. That's what a lot of men come in here looking for. So I thought I'd ask. I'd only do it if you thought you'd like it. Or it would help you—"

He held out his hand to shake. "My name's Larry," he said. "But I'm not gay. I've got a brother who's gay. His name is Steve. He's twenty-four—two years older than I am. He likes that stuff—guys sticking their dick up his ass. Sucking on guys' dicks. Once he asked me to pee in his mouth—that's a pretty funny thing to do for your brother. But I did it. He's still a nice guy, though. Now, you see, if Steve was here, you two would probably really like each other. But for me, I just need the

63

stimulation." Now he pulled his pants apart. "You want to play with my dick, you can do that." Circumcised, he was slightly smaller than average. "A strange guy, touching my penis—now *that's* stimulating. Like somebody staring at my ass."

So for the next twenty minutes I did, though he remained soft. We watched the movie, with a bit more desultory conversation, now about the hospital, now about his Connecticut family. A couple of more times he mentioned that Steve should be here. "But Steve's not nutzo like I am. He's just a real nice guy."

"When's the last time you ate?"

"Not since yesterday," he told me. "It's hard to get something to eat. Crowds make me lose it, and I always start to come apart . . . to drift. But people don't understand it when you're in a store with a lot of people, and you have to pull your pants down."

"I imagine that's a problem. I'm going out and bring back some food. What kind of sandwich would you like?"

"You're really going to go get something to eat—for me? Hey, that's awfully nice of you. Cheese. And mayonnaise. I don't really like meat. I'll eat it. But I don't really like it. Eating meat—that's *too* stimulating!" He grinned at me.

"Want a soda?"

"Sure. 7-Up. Sprite—just nothing with caffeine in it."

"Too stimulating?"

He laughed. "You're really a nice guy. You even sound like you understand me."

At that time it was only three dollars to get in to the Capri. Regularly I went out and bought food—sandwiches, soda, beer—for people in the theater. Mostly, though, it was for homeless men who were otherwise fairly together. The Capri's small, friendly Haitian manager and the security guard (who, after working there in uniform for three months, had switched back permanently to street clothes) still had a strict policy: no leaving and returning to the theater, without paying another entrance fee. When I said I was going out to get them some food, guys who knew the policy would often protest my going. "No, you can't do that. They'll make you pay again." I'd simply lie and tell them I was friends with the manager and that he'd let me back in for nothing. It added three dollars to the price of the sandwiches, the soda, the couple of apples, the piece of pastry, the container of yogurt, or the bananas from the Smilen's on the corner of Forty-fifth; but many of those guys needed that food.

When I came back into the theater with my paper bag from the deli, Larry—again naked—was getting up from the floor between the rows of seats, getting back into his T-shirt and filthy khaki slacks. He was grateful for the sandwich and soda. He stayed in his clothes for the next hour and only got up to show me his backside twice.

I left him shortly. Nor did I ever see him again. But I think it's something of a miracle that anyone in Larry's state could stay on the street even for the two days he'd been out of the hospital.

Given the twenty-five to thirty years I went to the various theaters, I don't believe I encountered a greater amount of madness in the movies than I did outside. But going there allowed me to see that madness from a different perspective—and perhaps learn a little about it. Among the dozen or so tales that I've let stand for the range of my encounters there—the many, many hundreds, indeed thousands, now briefer or more extended—the following story may loom large. But, unlike the representative tales before and after them, this one and Larry, and possibly forgetful Bobby, are the only cases of outright madness I encountered in the movies in a quarter of a century.

Certainly this is the most disturbing.

In the last months of the Variety Photoplays, before the city closed it in the late eighties, one October Saturday afternoon when I was again in the Variety's balcony, I heard from one of the forward rows a kind of rushed mumble, which now and then cleared into an audible exclamation: ". . . them fuckin' tits, man—oh, shit, them tits! Go on, sit on my face, bitch . . . Oh, fuckin' Jesus . . . !"

The man looked about twenty-five or twenty-six. He had very short hair—was, indeed, a skinhead *avant la lettre*. The five or six days' growth on his cheeks was the same length as the fuzz over his scalp. A dark short-sleeve shirt was open over his chest, as he twisted and bounced in his seat, down in the second row.

His gaunt arm's motion clearly told he was masturbating. The energy and animation recalled Joey-Who-Needs-a-Bath. But no one sat anywhere near him. Nor, in the next hour and a half, did he seem to achieve a climax. His mumble-and-shout went on and on as he bounced and twisted and flung himself about in his seat, pumping now with one hand, now, after twenty or forty minutes, switching to the other. He was beating at himself as vigorously when I left the theater as when I'd arrived.

That Friday night I was again at the Variety. When I came up the stairs into the balcony, again I heard that inarticulate mumble from down front.

Minutes on, my own curiosity was articulated by two guys near the wall:

"Who's that crazy man carrying on down front there?"

"Him? You mean the Mad Masturbator—that's what the guys here call him. He started coming here a couple of weeks ago. He's harmless though."

"He looks like he's . . . nuts!"

"Well, yeah—that, too."

In the theater that night I got into a couple of pleasant encounters, which I won't regale you with, but which, uncharacteristically, kept me there until the place closed, around one in the morning.

The picture shut down.

Around the wall, in pairs on their transformer boxes, cleaning lights came on.

Only five or six guys still sat. They lifted themselves out of the brown wood seats on their iron frames (as old as the seats in the elementary school that, in my first year there, had housed the Annex to the Bronx High School of Science), and walked toward the balcony's central aisle.

The only guy who didn't get up was the Mad Masturbator—still in the second row, who continued mumbling, continued masturbating, continued his thrashing and writhing. Curious, I lingered.

Down in the orchestra, one of the managers was shoving a pushbroom up the aisle. He stopped, leaned on his broom, looked up as though he already knew someone would be there, and called, "Come on—get out, Joe! Yeah, you! We're closing."

In the second row the man stood up (this time he wore a dark striped T-shirt), still pumping himself—and I saw: He wore no pants.

Bending down, he picked up a pair of Bermuda-length denim cut-offs from the floor. Now hopping, now staggering, now grabbing a chair arm—but without ceasing to masturbate for more than five or six seconds—he got them on. Lifting up a green knapsack, he swung that back over one arm and, holding his crotch—twisting and rubbing at it, through his pants—he came out to the aisle and started up for the stairway. The cut-offs were not closed, and one side hung down over a naked hip. He wore a pair of old loafers—and no socks. His feet and ankles were dirty. In the space before the stairway into the lobby, he stopped for a while, took his genitals out of his pants, and again began to pump his fist into his groin: ". . . those fuckin' tits, yeah . . . just sittin' on my face . . . yeah . . . like that, baby, the way to fuck me . . . man, them tits . . ."

Two other men went out around him—one glanced at him, one didn't. He bent over a couple of time, still pounding, stood, then bent again.

I thought he was going to climax.

But finally he pushed his genitals inside, his penis making a tent in the denim. Mumbling and clutching at it through his shorts, he started quickly down the steps.

My cap had fallen behind my seat, and when I found it, he'd gone. Downstairs I was the last person in the theater lobby. When I went outside, the Mad Masturbator was gone from the street.

I skipped next Saturday. But the Saturday after, I was back. When the guy on the stool tore my ticket, I asked him, "Do you know the guy who sits upstairs and . . . talks to himself?"

"You mean the crazy guy?"

"I guess so."

"Yeah, he's up there. He comes in here every day. He's in this place as soon as it opens. He's kind of a nuisance if you want to hear the movie—" He snorted. "But with these movies, guys don't come in here to listen. He don't hurt nobody."

"What's his story?" I asked.

The guy shrugged. The older man with the silver hair said, "He probably should be in a hospital." Then someone else came in, so I walked on across the lobby.

If you sat in the orchestra a few rows from the balcony's overhang and listened hard, you could just hear the mumbling susurrus above. I've said that odd behavior intrigues me. Somewhere in there I decided I was going to see if I could learn more about him.

I went upstairs, walked down to the front—he was there, frenetically, frantically working at himself, head moving left and right, talking to himself a mile a minute—and moved in between the seats till I was a seat away from him. His pants were gone. His feet were bare. A seat away lay his knapsack, and probably his cut-offs.

I leaned over the seat between us. "Excuse me . . . ? Excuse me . . . ?"

The "fuckin' tits" he was rhapsodizing over, while he pounded at his crotch were not, just then, on the screen. In *this* particular minute and a half of film, the stud hero and his comic sidekick were trying to break into the (wrong) woman's beach cottage.

"Eh . . . excuse me?"

His mumble stopped, though not his fist. He looked over at me and blinked. "Hey, am I making too much noise again? I'm sorry, man. I'll be quieter."

"That's okay. I just wanted to . . . know what your name was."

"My name . . . ?" He turned his bare knees toward me, as far as the seat arm would let him. In his lap his fist moved so fast it was invisible. His unshaven face strained. Through it, he managed: ". . . Joe . . . my name is Joe Marinsky . . ." or something very near it. Because of the perpetual motion of his arm, as I'd already noticed with his mumblings, when he spoke he sounded like a baritone Belinda Carlyle. "Joe Marinsky . . . what's yours?"

"My name is Chip," I said. "You know, a lot of people in here call you the—"

But he flung himself back and swung one knee wide from the other. "Oh, shit! I'm sorry . . . I gotta piss—" From his hard, circumcised penis, urine arched—in a stream narrow as a needle—only an inch and a half or two inches, to splatter down on his seat's edge. He pushed his bottom forward on the wood so that his pee would fall to the floor. "Oh, shit," he muttered, while his thin fingers—slowly now—climbed his erect shaft, then retreated, as slowly, into his sparse crotch hair. Pale and weak looking, his hand climbed again. "Jesus, I'm sorry . . . I got an empty milk carton I usually do it in. Then I pour it out, later, outside. They don't like it when I go on the floor like this. But sometimes it sneaks up on you, you know? Surprises you. But that's 'cause I was talking to you."

"No problem," I said. "When you got to go, you got to go."

His response to the archaic saw was a muttered "Jesus . . . " Over the next thirty seconds, the minuscule stream grew weaker, finally to dribble over his fist. He took away his hand long enough to wipe it on his shirt, clutched himself once more, and, sitting up, again began to pump full speed. "I get sores on my cock sometimes when I pee all over myself like that and I don't wash my hands."

I wasn't sure if he was explaining what *had* happened or what *would* happen. "Do you want me to go downstairs and get you some wet paper towels from the bathroom?" Maybe one day in three there were towels in the mirrored towel dispenser beside the sink in the downstairs john—the only john in the city, I believe, that still had a coin lock, into whose silver box you had to deposit a dime to get in.

"No, that's okay. I wiped my hand off pretty good. You're a faggot?"

"Yeah," I said, surprised by the word. "Actually, yes, I am."

"You wanna do something with me? Suck on it? Jerk me off for a while, maybe? I mean, sure, go on, if you want. Go ahead—that'd be great. Maybe I could get a little rest—some sleep, you know?" He turned back to the screen, still beating. "Oh, man, I wanna kiss on them big fuckin' tits . . . I just wanna . . . I want 'em all over me . . ." He looked at me again. "Come on, move over beside me. Sit here—and jerk on my dick for me. Hard, that'd be good. So I can get some fuckin' sleep."

I moved around the seat arm.

As soon as I took hold of him—he was small, bone hard, and instead of being warm like most hard cocks, his was actually cool—he took his hand away and shook his arm in front of him, like someone trying to get a cramp out, or to wake up a limb fallen asleep. He shook it once more. "Go on," he said. "Real hard. It's gotta be pretty hard or I can't feel it."

The skin on most cocks, no matter how much of a workout they get, is pretty soft. But his, head to hair, was thick, leathery, dry, like the skin on the ball of your foot. I gripped it tighter and began to rub.

Joe took a great breath, put his head back, and once more took up his soliloquy. Some thirty seconds into it, though, he closed his eyes. Ten seconds later, he ceased to mumble as his head fell to the side. His grip on the theater's iron chair arms loosened. After a minute, in the film's flicker, from the corner of his lips, a line of bright saliva wormed through the bronze hairs, down his jaw.

I couldn't believe he'd actually gone to sleep with someone jerking on his small, rocky dick. But a minute later, eyes still closed, he muttered something else about tits. Every few seconds over the next ten minutes, though his eyes stayed shut, his breath slow, and his body still, some obscenity bubbled blurrily from his mouth. Once his right hand jerked up, then fell again to his side. On his fuzzed jaw the saliva collected in a growing drop that didn't fall.

My hand was becoming tired, so I stopped.

Within seconds, his own hand crawled over his lap to grasp himself. As he started pumping, his eyes opened and, like someone waking on the couch after the national anthem is over, the flag has stopped waving, and the screen has played only confetti for twenty minutes, he blinked and lifted his head. "How much time . . . " He looked over at me again, beating. "How long did I sleep?" Beside me, again his body began to jerk.

I said, "About ten minutes." I'd been sure his "sleeping" was pretense, though I couldn't imagine the reason for it.

"Oh," he said. "Oh . . . it was still nice. One guy, I only saw him in here once. But he beat on it, sucked on it . . . he worked on me almost three whole *hours*, man. I got almost three whole hours sleep. Jesus, I felt so good after that—but even ten minutes, that's good. Thank you."

I asked, "Where do you stay when you're not in the theater?" I expected him to tell me he was homeless.

"I got a room, up by Stuyvesant Park. My parents pay for it—they'll pay for it as long as I don't bother them. Or get in *too* much trouble with the police. But I come in here every day, 'cause I don't bother so many people as I do when I'm just out on the street. Or in a regular movie. Or in the park. Sure, I bother *some* people in here. But not as many."

"Have you been to a doctor about . . . this?"

"Doctors? Oh, man, yeah. The last time they put me in the nut house, I thought they were going to throw away the damned key. But my parents said they'd take me—they don't really want me around. But they pay for my room. The doctors were talking about cutting some nerves inside my dick so I wouldn't feel *anything* when I choked my fucking chicken. Choking the chicken . . . ?" He looked down at himself. "I used to call it skinning my rabbit. Because I used to bleed all the time. Jesus, that's a mess. 'Cause then you can only rub it on one side. You ever do it so much you made it bleed?"

"No," I said. "No, I never did."

"Oh," he said. "Well, neither do I, no more—unless I get too much pee on it and don't wipe it clean." He shook his head. "I don't want 'em to cut no nerves. I mean, I'd do it anyway. I know that. 'Cause I don't really do it for the sex."

"You do it for the stimulation?"

"Huh . . . ?" He glanced over, wet lips shaking with his shaking fist. "Stimu-lation? What do you mean?"

"That's okay," I said. "Never mind."

"I do it 'cause I *have* to do it. That's all. But this way, at least every once in a while it actually *feels* good, if I haven't rubbed myself raw."

"Do you come?"

"Oh, yeah. I still come—every two or three weeks, I shoot a *nice* load." His eyes went back to the screen, where the wrong woman and the right one were in the midst of a lesbian scene, while the hero hid in a closet, looking through the crack, and the sidekick, peeking in from outside the window, tried to get his at-tention and mime to him that the villain was getting closer and closer, while try-ing not to be seen by the women making languorous love. "Just like any normal guy. I ain't so big, but I shoot me a good load every couple of weeks. It hurts like a motherfucker sometimes, but I still like to do it . . . Oh, baby, yeah, eat that fuck-ing pussy . . . " Again he glanced back at me. "I had a girl once—this summer? She picked me up in the park. She found me, when I was in the bushes, doing it like now. I asked, and she said she'd come back to my room with me. I fucked her and fucked her and fucked her, man. Then I fucked her some more. I thought she liked me and was going to stay around for a while. But the next day she left. She said I made her sore. I was sore too. But that's another reason I come into this place. I thought it was 'cause my parents had me cut that I did it so much. I didn't have no protection on my cock. But most of the guys in here are cut too—and they don't do it as much as me. I wonder why that is? Anyway. When I do it here with my hands, I can control the pressure better. And my dick doesn't hurt so much."

A few minutes later, when I left him, Joe had changed hands from left to right and was deep into his own hallucinated inner movie, while the one in the theater rolled its credits down the screen, intertwining actual and invented names: Written and produced by Billy Thornberg, Director of photography Junior "Speedy" Bodden, Key grip Randy Wanker, Make-up by Ruby Midnight, Edited by Erica English and Christopher Haven, Art director Pez D. Spencer . . .

During the next few months, Joe was already there every time I arrived; he was always there when I left—as much a fixture as the old man in the Venus. Two or three times people moved in to have sex with him. A few people even said a regular "Hello" when they came in. By and large, though, he was left alone. Most of the customers, I believe, he frightened. For Joe's derangement—the Mad Masturbator's stooped shoulders, his scrawny arms, his drooling, incontinent satyriasis like something loosed babbling from the sealed cellars of a Victorian madhouse—was such that, if only from his avatars, persistent in nineteenth-century and early twentieth-century texts on masturbation, from William Acton to Colonel Kellogg and L. L. Nunn, you couldn't help wondering if Joe was where, in some way, we were all going. The answer was, however, the hundreds on hundreds I met there, who, whatever strangenesses we displayed, and often with sexualities even more intense than Joe's, were not in any way like him—nor at all like Larry.

Two months later the city closed the Variety Photoplays—the second oldest functioning theater building in New York—when city inspectors noted (ran an article in the *Daily News*) "a hundred-fifty-eight acts of unsafe sex," while further west on Fourteenth Street the green shell of Luchow's restaurant and the Academy of Music (more recently the Palladium) were already or soon to be condemned. What accommodations, if any, Joe was able to make for his condition, I cannot even imagine.

VI

It seems somewhat lunatic to write about what I saw in the more than half dozen commercial porn theaters I frequented over thirty years without some discussion of the movies themselves, at least for two or three pages—for basically what I saw over those decades was thousands and thousands of hours of pornographic film and videotape, aimed at a heterosexual male audience. That amounts to thousands of titles. In the first third of this period, this meant seeing many of these films three, five, even seven or eight times, either because I had chosen to spend six or seven hours at the movies that day, or because the theaters brought the films back almost at random when a new title was delayed or unavailable. With such extensive exposure, certainly I and the rest of the regular audience were desensitized to certain aspects of the films. But by the same token I suspect I was highly sensitized to certain others—specifically those aspects that constituted the films as a genre (or, better, their several subgenres). Also I think I am fairly well informed as to the response to them by the general straight male audience who saw them with me during those years. Hyperbole is the rhetorical mode in which Americans traditionally speak about their common and garden variety filmic experiences. Certainly I have not escaped that rhetoric here. Still, however clumsily—or even inaccurately—I may put it, something needs to be said about the films as films over those thirty years.

The first decade focused on those screen movies with plots, however hokey. Some of those films, however, were quite ingenious, such as *Baby Face* (1977). Released a year or so later in a horrendously cut-up version as *Hot Daughter*, it's difficult to find today unmutilated. In its pristine form, however, it's an extraordinary gender reversal saga. From seducing various of her teachers, a horny schoolgirl comes down to the river to get laid with a dockhand she meets there. When, accompanied by her mother, the police discover them, the dockworker flees. Running from the cops, he falls into the water, where, having been knocked unconscious and carried downstream, he's rescued by some beautiful women. To hide from the girl's vengeful mom he has to work in the women's male brothel, catering to rich, successful women: a stockbroker, a dress designer, a racing car driver . . . The mother, herself a client at the place, traces him there, however. There's a gang-bang scene, when the racing driver, triumphant and celebrating after her latest victory, demands an orgy from the owners, that's extraordinary. Things climax with some incredible S&M hugger-mugger, including the immobilization of our hero in saran wrap, all except his genitals. To escape castration at the mother's hands, he has to hop around the brothel, privates flapping, as the place is raided by the police. *Baby Face* won its director, Alex de Renzy, an award for best direction of an erotic film that year. I found it one of the most interesting—and funniest— films of its decade, whether porn or legit. Jack Wrangler's comedy *Jack and Jill*, with the delightful Samantha Fox, while it does not have the (yes) intellectual richness of *Baby Face*, is still a wonderfully American film. The trials and tribulations of the marvelously naive couple of New York yuppie swinging singles (with a bit of Nick and Nora Charles thrown in) are rich and well observed. The film is one of the few sex comedies that's both sexy *and* funny.

These and like commercial porn films (*Lickety Split, Mount of Venus, Roller Babies, Barbara Broadcast*—the last is *much* better than its title, while the others are much worse . . .) employed a recognizable stable of actors and actresses.

What made a good male porn star was not much different from what made a good male ballet partner. You had to be strong and keep it hard to keep the scene going. Regularly, when she was mouthing your dick, you pulled her hair back so the guys could see her face. You moved her arm or her leg—*gently!*—from between the action point and the camera.

The quick take, I suppose, is that while the makers of these movies wanted the males to be emblematically masculine (the big dicks), they didn't want them to be threatening as personalities. But I think things were more complicated than that. You also had to have something that allowed the good time *you* were having to extend and amplify the feminine sexuality that was, after all, what the guys were paying to see: That manifested itself in a kind of male androgyny. At any rate, that's what Holmes had. Mark ("Mr. Ten-and-a-Half") Stevens had it too. Stevens did as many gay films as he did straight ones. (Once I saw him get out of a taxi on Eighth Street with Annie Sprinkle and a couple of other actors, in the rain. He died early from AIDS.) Paul Thomas had it. When he played against it, as he did in his role as one of the male prostitutes in the extraordinary *Baby Face*, servicing the masochistic black dress designer, Negra, the results (because he could never efface it completely) were uncanny. Thomas went on to do some intelligent directing. And Jack Wrangler had it—another switch hitter between gay and straight.

John Holmes, for example, was not *just* a fourteen-inch schlong (which made him an all but household name between 1976 and his death from AIDS in 1988—three years after having been involved in a multiple drug murder that, with his illness, pretty much ended his career). Rather, Holmes was a fourteen-inch schlong on one of the gentlest, yet wholly self-confident heterosexual males imaginable. At least that's how his film presence registered. When the script for his continuing character, "Johnny Wadd," called for him to defeat and subdue criminals, or even to shout, he never raised his voice above mild surprise. His slender arms, manicured nails, and huge . . . gold ring, which he wore in film after film, put him only a step away from the effeminate.

At once supermasculine and all but androgynous, Holmes, the man with the largest public dick in America, had secured his first job in porn from the woman who roomed next to him in college, and had gone into it for a lark. The heterosexual male audience was fascinated by this guy in whom the usual boundary between the desire to be him and the desire to possess him was set so intriguingly (in male heterosexual terms) askew.

To this gay viewer who, over thirty years, saw hundreds and hundreds of these things with a largely straight male audience sitting in the dark around me, this ambiguity seems the *sine qua non* for any sort of popular success as a male porn star. One or two succeeded without it, through having the next best thing—a boyish friendliness (Harry Reems, Joey Silvera [a.k.a. Civera]) toward the actresses that, yes, in some of the others broke down into a kind of half-belligerent bullying (Ron Jeremy and, later, T. T. Boy). But the straight audience was there to see the women.

Let me point out: Personally, I find these guys, all of them, absolutely *without* sex appeal. Slender, waspy, willowy, understated, they are insistently amasculine, but this is what a successful *male* porn star needed in the realm of straight films during the 1970s, unless like Jeremy, Reems, or Wrangler, he lapsed beefily into the comic. There were some wonderfully wacky women: Annie Sprinkle, Candy Samples, Christy Canyon. Others, like Sharon Kane, R. D. Liang, Aunt Peg, Gloria Leonard, the extraordinary actress Georgina Spelvin—and Samantha Fox—had something even more valuable as sexual partners. They were personable. They came off in part after part as intelligent women (whatever the bizarre situation they found themselves in during this film or that) who had fun with sex.

And Vanessa del Rio deserves a book-length study and celebration all her own.

There were directors with a certain style, like Gerard Damiano. Bob Chinn did a barely adequate job with Holmes's Johnny Wadd series, managing to give a few of them some memorable moments. Endless others were jaw droppingly bad. But that made the few good ones that much more interesting. Among the notable directors, actress/director Jennifer Welles, when she was over forty, made films about sexy forty-plus-year-old women. And Gloria Leonard became a pretty interesting producer.

While the films were often financed indirectly (or directly) by organized crime, a good number of the working technicians, writers, and actors were the disaffected brothers and sisters and cousins and aunts and uncles of the Jewish New

Left. Without intending to be, these movies represented a tremendous sexual education for their working-class audience—in the case of New York City, mostly Hispanic, black, and Catholic white. The "sex act" as far as these films were concerned was a four-part affair, starting with fellatio, going on to cunnilingus, then with some female-superior action, and (perhaps after a bit of "doggie style" thrown in) a male-superior finish, with a pull-out cum shot all over her face, tits, ass, belly, or whatever—and ending with a gentle, lingering kiss, often on the actress's cum-streaked lips.

Generally, I suspect, pornography improved our vision of sex all over the country, making it friendlier, more relaxed, and more playful—qualities of sex that, till then, had been often reserved to a distressingly limited section of the better-read and more imaginative members of the mercantile middle classes.

For the first year or two the theaters operated, the entire working-class audience would break out laughing at everything save male-superior fucking. (I mean, that's *what* sex is, isn't it?) At the fellatio, at the cunnilingus even more, and at the final kiss, among the groans and chuckles you'd always hear a couple of "*Yuccchs*" and "*Uhggggs*." By the seventies' end, though, only a few chuckles sounded out now—at the cunnilingus passages. And in the first year or two of the eighties, even those had stopped. (No, *that's* what sex is: a four-part act, oral and genital, where everybody gets a chance to be on top. Anything *else* was what was weird.) Indeed, I think, under pressure of those films, many guys simply found themselves changing what turned them on. And if one part or another didn't happen to be your thing, you still saw it enough times to realize that maybe *you* were the strange one, and it behooved you to sit it out politely and put up with it, unless you wanted people to think *you* were strange.

The movies presented a world in which a variety of heterosexual and lesbian acts were depicted regularly, even endlessly, in close-up detail. The only perversion that did not exist in their particular version of pornotopia, save for the *most* occasional comic touches (and even these would still get a groan from the audience as late as '86 or '87), was male homosexuality. But its absence from the narrative space on the screen proper is what allowed it to go on rampantly among the observing audience, now in this theater, now in that one. And, if I have to make it explicit, the majority of that was guys like me who enjoyed sucking cock for our own pleasure, fellating other guys who were getting off on the straight screen action. Guys in drag and makeup (sometimes) did it for a few bucks. Guys like me in jeans and work shirts did it for fun. My sense was that the occasional jokes about the competition between us were a sign of just how little competition there actually was. Some men moved back and forth, but generally the ones who wanted to pay, the ones who didn't, and the ones who just wanted to be left alone made three pretty distinct groups.

One of the truths the makers of these early films got hold of and were able to exploit until cheap video obliterated the film market was that, paradoxical as it seems, most straight men do *not* fantasize about sex with *women* so much as they fantasize about sex with *secretaries, nurses, waitresses, prostitutes, women doctors, women's magazine editors, schoolgirls, movie actresses* seen on the screen, *housewives* and *businesswomen* passed in the street.

Once, when WAP (Women Against Pornography) was leading its tours through the area in the early eighties, I did an informal tabulation of six random commercial porn films in the Forty-second Street area and six random legit movies playing around the corner in the same area during the same week. I counted the number of major female characters portrayed as having a profession in each: the six legit films racked up seven (one had three, one had zero). The six porn films racked up eleven. On the same films I took tabs on how many friendships between women were represented, lesbian or otherwise, in the plot. The six legit films came out with zero; the six porn films came out with nine. Also: How many of each ended up with the women getting what they wanted? Five for the porn. Two for the legit.

Was commercial film pornography sexist? Certainly. Was it anywhere near as sexist as the legit films playing across the nation's screens in the same years? Not unless you simply took sexist and sexy as synonyms.

The twenty-five to thirty years that make up the history of the commercial pornographic theaters took me from age twenty-five to age fifty-five. I went into those years a man perceived as more or less young. I came out of them a man perceived (at least by folks in their twenties) as more or less old. At the start of my thirties I was a gay single father, raising a daughter in the city, making my living as a freelance writer. Today I am a professor of comparative literature, eight years into a rewarding relationship with another man. That transition we call, in our society, adulthood.

It was not a static period. Energies, interests, and the workings of the body shift almost as much over those years as they do between five and thirty-five.

But more than one person grew up with the pornographic sex theaters.

My first memory of Jonathan is somewhat blurred. But it was in the Capri. I recall a young guy, sitting down front on the right, masturbating and watching the movie. I remember it was fairly late at night, and when I sat next to him, there was a conversation. "What's your name?"

"Jonathan."

"How old are you, John?"

"It's Jonathan. I'm twenty."

"You look like a kid."

"Yeah, I know. Everybody tells me that. I just look young. But I'm twenty. Really."

"How long have you been coming here?"

A shrug. "A couple of years. Three, four . . ."

"I'm surprised I never saw you before."

And when we got down to sex, everything I did to him, five minutes later he did to me—unusual enough to note in the general exchanges in the theater.

Once I spotted him ambling through the neighborhood outside and for the hell of it followed him, till he turned in to a pinball and video arcade up on Broadway.

A much clearer memory of him comes from '86, the year I was a visiting fellow at Cornell University's Society for the Humanities. Coming back to the city on some brief business, I stopped in to the movies. At this point Jonathan was wearing a black leather jacket, rare enough in the theater to note. The sex was sweaty, mutual, and memorable. Afterward the conversation drifted to his interest in a two-year college program and my classes up at Ithaca. Before I left, I'd acquired the nickname "professor." Half a dozen years later, I would have said that *all* these memories were from the same year or two . . . Over the next few, though, when I ran into Jonathan, he always greeted me with a friendly "Hi, professor!" And once, in '92 or '93 when I'd actually *been* a professor for the last four years, teaching at the University of Massachusetts, while Jonathan and I were talking and he was telling me about the ins and outs of his superintendent job in an East Side apartment building, he called me "Professor Delany."

I frowned. "Did I ever actually tell you my last name?"

"No." He laughed. "But I've been seeing your picture in the papers, and on books and things for—Jesus, more than ten years now. I've known who you are for a *long* time."

I frowned. "How old *are* you now, Jonathan?"

"Thirty."

Now I laughed. "Are you married yet? Do you have a family going?"

"Me?" He chuckled. "Are you kidding? *You* got a daughter, I know. But I'm as gay as a plaid rabbit."

"Oh—!"

Jonathan was a quintessentially butch-looking number.

"You're really *thirty*?" I laughed again. "That means we've known each other at least ten years!"

Now it was Jonathan who laughed. "We've known each other a good deal longer than *that*, professor. I remember, I met you the third time I came in this place—and the first three times were all in the first week I learned about it."

"And . . . how old were you when you first came in here?"

He gave me a sly look. "Fifteen."

"Oh, come on!" I said. "Don't tell me that! You mean to say, I had sex with you when you were fifteen years *old*?"

"Several times. Somebody gave me this phony identification. All my friends thought I was going to use it to drink. But about the only thing I wanted to do with it was see the dirty movies. I used to tell everybody here I was twenty—and that I'd been coming here for years. The first few times I came in here, I was scared to death. I didn't know *what* the fuck was going on. So I just did everything I saw anybody else do. I'd come in here and see somebody with his dick out, beatin' off. I'd take *my* dick out and beat off. Somebody would come along and suck on my dick. I'd turn around and suck on his. And I tell you, it was fuckin' wonderful! Everybody was so nice. I mean, I was just a kid. The guys in here could have chewed me up and spit me out back then. But they didn't. I remember I met one guy in here one evening who had an extra ticket to a Broadway show because somebody he was supposed to go with had canceled out, so he took *me* instead! My first Broadway play—I was maybe seventeen. Just like that, an hour after he met me. Then, a week later, he got us some tickets to a concert up at Lincoln Center and he took me to *that*, too. The show was fun, but the concert was fuckin' *amazing*! I still go to concerts, every chance I get. And you told me all about applying up at Manhattan Community College—how I didn't have to be scared of all the classes, because there'd be advisors there to help me with my schedule. I didn't know any of that shit! I thought you had to do that all yourself. You gave me your phone number and told me I could call you up if I had any problems. You said your name was Chip or something."

"I did?" I had no memory of it. But certainly it's the sort of thing I'd do with any young person I was discussing school with.

"Yeah. The same month, I saw an article about you in the papers, and it had your picture and everything. Once I called up the number you gave me, and your answering machine said it was really you, with your voice. So I told people you were a friend of mine—only I didn't tell them where I knew you from. But that was kind of cool. I mean, I learned half the stuff I *know* in this place. People told me here how not to get AIDS—and I sure don't got it. I get tested just about every year. You do too, professor—you told me that."

"I do," I said. "I mean, I did?"

"Yeah!"

Later, walking up half a dozen bus stops, I recalled my own first visit to Forty-second Street—yes, at about age fifteen. I wondered what it would have been like if the sex movies had existed then and been an option for me. I tried to imagine what it might have been like, coming into this darkened public space of public sex for the first time at fifteen, sixteen, seventeen . . .

There may be as many ideal sex lives as there are different people. As a general template, I've always felt my best when I had a single person in my life as a sexual focus, at the same time a general population of encounters with different men (of the sort I've been describing here), along with a healthy masturbatory life. But what made that a feasible way to live between 1975 and 1995 were institutions such as the sex movies, the baths, and the bars like the Mineshaft and the Vault with grope rooms and "sex lounges." For me, however, the movies were the most important.

Even after I'd had my picture in the *Village Voice* or the *Advocate* a fair number of times and now and again in the gay press, Jonathan is the only person who's *told* me he recognized me in the theater. Once, though, as I came into the Capri three days after I'd taped a show for PBS, a tall black guy, Eddy, stopped me with a hand on my shoulder and said, "Hey, there—now was that you, a couple of nights back, interviewed on *Charlie Rose*?"

I turned, trying to look my most bemused. "You mean on television? Me? Aw, come on, Eddy. If I was somebody on television, what would I be doing in a place like this?"

"Oh, now," he objected, "we got some very famous people comin' in here." He named a sixties/seventies pop singer who, actually, I'd seen and spoken with there a number of times, but whom, though he still did his share of oldies concerts, had fallen out of fame's spotlight so that he could now go where he wanted and do what he liked. Then Eddy named a movie star who was *so* famous, I just laughed. If such a person *had* set foot in the Capri, the queens in the back row would have been chattering about it for the next six months. As they were our own information superhighway, all the semi-hemi-demi-regulars at the theater would have known.

Even now, a queen nearby overheard us, pulled himself out of the conversation with the person beside him, and turned to face the aisle. Drawing up to look around, he demanded, "Where? Where, honey? *Oooohh*! Show him to me! *Where is he?*"

A final portrait from the Capri's last year may make a few final points. Rannit was a stolid, good-looking East Asian, his black hair cut marine short. I first saw him in 1994, working the corner of Forty-fifth Street, in a navy pea jacket, an orange advertising bib strapped over it, front and back. He was snapping out purple leaflets into the hands of passersby, for a strip club blocks north.

A couple of days later, in the Capri, when I was coming down the aisle, I saw him sitting back off to the side, jacket in the chair against the wall, knees wide and up against the backs of the two seats ahead of him, slacks unzipped, masturbating. When I slowed, he looked up at me with a welcoming smile—so I slid in to the seat beside him. The sex was protracted and friendly. The man was

Shortly after the city closed the theater, in October 1996 the marquee of the Capri still jutted over the east side of Eighth Avenue just before Forty-sixth Street and north of a parking lot. In 1998 the building was completely renovated and the theater space demolished. It opened again as the Starstruck Restaurant.

as naturally affectionate as Tommy. Twenty minutes later, when sex gave way to conversation, I learned that Rannit was twenty-eight and lived with his mother in the Bronx. His English was without accent, as he'd come to this country at age two. In Rannit's jacket pocket was a paperback novel, bought from a street vendor for fifty cents three days back, that he'd just finished reading that afternoon: Kurt Vonnegut's *Slaughterhouse Five*. And he'd read all the Robert Anton Wilson *Illuminati* books and been amused by them. Unlike most of the audience, he knew the names of the actors in the films the Capri was showing: "They should bring back some of those old Vanessa del Rio films. She was the greatest. I mean, *there* was a porn star who really knew how to be sexy." It's a judgment most connoisseurs of heterosexual porn from the seventies and early eighties agree is a sign of taste. "I got a collection of them I keep in my closet, so my mom doesn't know I have them."

Whenever I passed him giving out flyers on the corner, he always had a smile and a surprised "Hello!" He was always glad to see me in the theater. His analysis of the problems of the place were to the point: "You know, if you sit in the dark where nobody can see what you're doing, hardly anybody comes by to sit with you. And I never would have met you, see? But when you *do* sit under a light and let everybody see, then it scares some of the guys away. I think they think I'm probably crazy or something. I mean, you see 'em. They look, then they turn and run off. Maybe they think I want money. But sometimes you can sit there ten, fifteen minutes, a half an hour, pullin' on yourself before somebody'll get up the nerve to sit down and do you. And most of the time I come in here, I only got my lunch hour, I can't hang around after work 'cause I gotta go home and eat." Rannit dropped out of high school in his junior year, then got a GED. Had he ever considered going to college, I asked. (He's as sharp or sharper than any number of my B or even AB students up at U. Mass.) I'm about the third or fourth person who's suggested it to him, he admits. But when would he have the time? He has to work and help out his mom.

One day, as I was about to leave the theater, I mentioned to Rannit I was going to get a slice of pizza. About to leave himself, he explained, he was thinking the same thing. "Come on," I suggested. "Let's go." We walked up the aisle together, nodded to the Haitian security man standing in the lobby talking with the Haitian manager, and left.

In the seventy-five-yard walk that took us to the corner of Forty-fifth Street, across Eighth Avenue, and down the street to Ray's—the first time I'd been with him when he wasn't working or in the movies—Rannit managed to brush up against three women on the street, dragging his hand across their hip as he passed, and, once, as he was going into the pizza place, outright grabbing a young woman's behind. She turned and gave him a sharp, disgusted look. He grinned at her, then at me.

As we were eating our pizza, rather appalled, I told him, "Rannit, if you're interested in getting to women, grabbing ass like that on the street is *probably* not the best way to do it!"

After swallowing a mouth full of pizza, he said with his open smile, "Huh . . .?"

I said, "No woman's going to give you the time of day if you go around acting like that!"

Again he said, ". . . Huh?"

"Look." I took another tack. "If you're really interested in getting that nice, hard dick of yours up some real, wet, sloppy pussy, there are a lot better ways to go about getting yourself laid than—"

A woman passed by our table and, without looking away from me, Rannit dropped his hand off the edge and swung it down to brush her calf, as, with her tray, she hurried to the red masonite garbage receptacle at the door. I reached across and punched Rannit—playfully—in the shoulder.

"—than *that!*" I concluded.

Rannit's smile only brightened. "Huh?"

"You know—" I sighed—"you're going to get in trouble. What happens when some woman calls the police on you?"

A question worked into Rannit's smile. "Yeah, the cops are always hassling you when you do that stuff. Why do they *do* that?" For a moment I thought he was kidding.

"Because it's against the *law,*" I told him, "for one thing. You wouldn't like it either if somebody was always trying to cop a feel off you wherever you went!"

Brightly, curiously, he repeated, "Huh?"

Friendly, affectionate, good-looking, moderately intelligent Rannit is what most people, working-class and up, would designate in our society as a "creep." But I hadn't known it till then.

Rannit operates outside an entire discourse of "normal" male/female relationships (as he operates entirely within another). It has nothing to do with whether the rhetoric was vulgar or formal. I'd already noted, some weeks back, that while he knew what they meant and didn't mind if I used them, Rannit's well-spoken self-presentation was devoid of four-letter words.

As of yet I don't know whether or not his "Huh's?" were disingenuous, but an entire set of concepts seemed unknown to him. They just weren't there to make a range of possible statements that one could say to him make sense.

Rannit's a guy I'm unlikely to invite to my house. But that still doesn't mean that the sex between us wasn't fulfilling and mutually satisfying. And, who knows: If we continue running into each other the way we have as long as, say, I've been running into Tommy or any one of a dozen others, maybe I'll be a good influence. Perhaps I'll begin to get across to him some idea that there are other ways to behave in this society that might satisfy the largely heterosexual components of his desire, ways that are a good deal more socially acceptable than touching up women in the street. Next time we met, when I pressed him, he admitted that this behavior had once gotten him his wrist cracked by a policeman's nightstick when he was seventeen, gotten him pushed back up against lots of brick walls and back fences, and into regular fights with protesting brothers and boyfriends and husbands, and repeatedly slapped by his mother, all through his early adolescence—before he learned to be more secretive and hide the activity better.

Jonathan learned "half" of what he knew in the movies. Certainly I'd learned a lot. Is it a place where someone like Rannit might be socialized out of an annoying habit? It took me another dozen "Huh's?" to determine that his habits seemed a cross between social and obsessive, rather than in any way directly sexually gratifying: "That's what I go to the *movies* for! Trying to cop a feel, that's just what guys *do*, ain't it? I see *lots* of other guys do it."

.   .   .

Other people have chronicled other facets of the neighborhood—the transsexual bars, the hard-core hustling scene (male and female), the heterosexual peep show life. But this was *my* Times Square. Along with the theaters on or around Fourteenth Street—Variety Photoplays, the Metropolitan, the Jefferson, the Academy of Music—and half a dozen others before them or contemporary with them for shorter or longer periods (including the Metro on 101st Street and Broadway, the Thalia on West Ninety-fifth Street, the Globe on East Tremont, and more recently, since the city shutdown, the Montauk in Passaic or the Spring Valley Adult), these were the social institutions that have seen me this far through my adulthood, as they saw Jonathan through his adolescence and young manhood. They have ushered me to the portals of old age, as much a part of my growth and maturation as any other institution in the city.

The encounters you remember are, of course, the men who were a little different, a little strange, the odder denizens of the Venus, this particular cock, that particular smile. Yes, they include the walking wounded, like Rannit. But most of the guys I had at the Capri, day in and day out, year after year (the professional medical companion whose wife had lupus: "So she doesn't want any sex at all, right now. And guys, girls, it never bothered me. She knows I come here. I think she prefers that to me going with other women—not that I go into the details about it with her"; fat, friendly, uncut Puerto Rican Tony, a Saturday morning regular down at the Variety for five years; the tree service worker there with his uncle, "'Cause he knew about this place—and we both like guys"; the tall, rather elegant black man at the Capri who never seemed to do much in the line of sex, but who always lingered standing at the back of the aisle, sometimes chatting with the clutch of black queens who commandeered the seats at the back-left of the orchestra, and who always had some bit of gossip for me when I came in, who always whispered, "Stay healthy, now," when I left. Perhaps because of some forgotten bit of conversation I'd overheard him in, years ago, I'd always called him "Eddy," until, one day, he looked at me curiously and smiled.

89

"Why do you call me 'Eddy'? That's not my name. I don't mind. But why you always call me that?"—though he wouldn't tell me what his name was when I apologized. "No, you just go on with Eddy. Maybe it's something sexual with you—no problem. Really, it's all right." The big, pear-shaped diabetic who always wore dress slacks and a white shirt: "When I got the diabetes, they said I wasn't going to be interested in sex no more. But you and me, we been seeing each other in here, *how* many years now?" The social worker taking night classes, whose papers I would correct, first in the light of the flickering screen, then, two years later, over the phone: "I'm an exhibitionist, man. I know it. Till I found this place, I used to get in trouble. But I can come in here, stand in the middle of the aisle, facing everybody, jerk off—and maybe a *couple* of guys call out, 'Hey, there! Sit down!' That's all. And most of you guys tell me you even get off on it. That's all I'm looking for, man"), though they tended to be more working-class than not, were pretty much like you, pretty much like me.

Were the porn theaters romantic? Not at all. But because of the people who used them, they were humane and functional, fulfilling needs that most of our society does not yet know how to acknowledge.

The easy argument already in place to catch up these anecdotes is that social institutions such as the porn movies take up, then, a certain social excess—are even, perhaps, socially beneficial to some small part of it (a margin outside the margin). But that is the same argument that allows them to be dismissed—and physically smashed and flattened: They are relevant only to that margin. No one else cares.

Well, in a democracy, that is not an acceptable argument. People are not excess. It is the same argument that dismisses the needs of blacks, Jews, Hispanics, Asians, women, gays, the homeless, the poor, the worker—and all other margins that, taken together (people like you, people like me), are the country's overwhelming majority: those who, socioeconomically, are simply less powerful.

·   ·   ·

Till 1985 public sex was largely a matter of public decency—that is to say, it was a question of who was or who wasn't offended by what went on in public venues. Since '85, for the first time, under a sham concern for AIDS, the acts themselves have been made illegal, even if done *with* condoms in a venue where *everyone* present approves. In October '95, after issuing endless contradictory statements about AIDS, the city gave all the theaters in the area a year—till this month, October '96—to be out, so that the renovations could get under way. The owner of the Eros lives on an upper floor in the building—which has delayed its closing, but only by another couple of months. Three months ago, five months ago, ten months ago, patrons walked up to the theaters to find the gates down over the glass, the ticket sellers' booth shadowed and vacant. We turned away, disappointed, curious—but they've been closed since. It *is* October '96, and, except for the Eros, all today are shut.

What makes their shutdown *so* troubling is that even as the city spoke of supporting "safer sex," while it hasn't made "being a homosexual" a crime, in the course of closing such places, by law it has *criminalized each and every homosexual act* (as well as masturbation and vaginal intercourse: straight sex clubs have fared no better) "in public" (a concept left hopelessly undefined), safe or unsafe, with *or* without a condom.[1] Although it's received far less publicity, and has even been supported by some gay men and women, this situation is potentially more serious than the 1992 Colorado referendum denying gays any special legal protection (later overturned by the Supreme Court).

Safe-sex-shmafe-sex, the city wanted to get the current owners out of those movie houses, "J/O Clubs" (Jack Off Clubs, advertised as just that on the marquees), and peep shows, and open up the sites for developers. Take a walk through. If you have any memory of what was there before, you'll see they've been largely

1. For details, see the extraordinary volume, *Policing Public Sex: Queer Politics and the Future of AIDS Activism,* edited by Dangerous Bedfellows (Ephen Glenn Colter, Wayne Hoffman, Eva Pendleton, *et al.*) (Boston: South End Press, 1996).

successful. Legally, however, they've set gay liberation back to a point notably *pre*-Stonewall. The talk now is of rezoning all such businesses over to the waterfront, while Forty-second Street proper will basically be a mall.

VII

Despite the many days I spent there, for well over half the clientele—and for me during *well* over three-quarters of my own visits—the sex movies were places where, for the admission price, if you knew what you were looking for and weren't too choosy, you could be in and out in forty minutes, more or less satisfied. Sure, you *could* spend a whole day. But that's not how most people used them—most of the time.

By comparison, bars are leisurely places where one passes an afternoon, an evening. You go there to meet people, to talk. If you're lucky, sometimes you'll find someone you like well enough to go home with. Or, if you're like me, a bar is a place to drop in after an hour at the movies, to have a drink, and maybe make some notes in your notebook before you go home.

Stella's is a gay bar east of Eighth Avenue on Forty-seventh. Though I've patronized it since it opened, only once, out of curiosity, have I ever gone home with somebody I met there—a long-haired, rather out-of-place-looking fellow from the Southwest with a swastika among the tattoos on his cabled forearms, which he swore up and down was a stupid adolescent mistake, he didn't have an anti-Semitic bone in his body, he wanted to have it removed. One of the butcher men I've ever met, once home he had me shove large objects into his butt, which made him flail, whinny, and shoot like a son of a bitch. I barely raised a hard. So, for me, Stella's is just a comfortable place for an afternoon drink.

On Tuesdays, Wednesdays, Fridays, and Saturdays, the daytime bartender is Jimmy Withrow. The list of the now vanished places Jimmy has worked is

Opening first as Trix on the old site of O'Neill's Backyard on Forty-eighth Street in the early 1980s, this bar moved to Fiftieth Street, beside a parking lot behind the actors' church, St. Malachi's. Then, changing its name to Stella's, it moved in the beginning of 1996 to its current site on Forty-seventh Street across from the closed-down Biltmore Theater.

a roster of the history of the neighborhood's gay bars: Walter's Pub, Guilda Grape, Something Special, the Turnstile, O'Neill's Backyard, La Fiesta, Dirty Edna's, and three incarnations of Trix. Did you ever work in the Haymarket, I asked.

"When I was a callow youth, perhaps I worked *out* of the Haymarket a few times. But, no." Jimmy chuckled. "I never worked there as a bartender." Jimmy has the longest unbroken record of work of any bartender in the midtown West Side gay bars. I first met him sometime in the seventies. Someone pointed him out, back then, as "Jimmy the Widow." Now and again you hear the nickname even today. How did he get it?

James Withrow at Stella's is the longest-working bartender among the West Side gay bars in the Forty-second Street area.

"Twenty-eight years ago, when I used to commute in from New Jersey, my first bartending job was across the street from a hotel. I started keeping a room there. Often, the fellows I'd take in with me didn't have anywhere to stay, so after we were finished I'd let them use the room for the night. I'd go back to Jersey. In the bar, people used to look out the window; they'd see me take some guy in. A few hours later, I'd come out—alone. What happened to the guy? Was I *eating* them, they wanted to know." Jimmy winked at me. "But it got to be a joke: 'The black widow strikes again!'" How did Jimmy feel about the Times Square changeover? "I welcome it," he declared. "The current shutdown hasn't changed our business—but business is certainly down from what it was, say, ten or fifteen *years* ago. Sure: The place where I used to grope sailors in the balcony is now a children's theater. But that's one of life's little ironies. In 1980, people would be two deep at the bar by eight o'clock in the morning. Now we don't open till noon." What brought about the change? "Drugs—and AIDS. And if they get the drugs out, I'm all for it." When Jimmy says drugs, doesn't he basically mean crack and coke? "Yeah. Heroin was never a big part of the gay scene, at least at the bar level. Heroin addicts don't cruise—their libidos don't work. You've been talking to hustlers out on the street? Then you've seen it. Kids running around like crazy men, looking for anything they can get. They can't keep steady customers. They're too strung out and at loose ends." (If not Darrell, that's certainly Dave.) "You remember in the fifties and sixties—Forty-second Street was a twenty-four hour neighborhood. More than a dozen double feature movies played till four in the morning—and opened at eight A.M. Half a dozen eating places—Grant's, Romeo's, Bickford's—were open all night long. There was even an all-night bookstore. I remember when there were public ashtrays and *trees* on Forty-second Street. If they get the drugs out of this neighborhood, we'll all benefit."

As a sign system, what the neon visibility of sex shops and peep shows and porn theaters signaled to people passing by was: Unattached men (or men whose attachments are, however temporarily, not uppermost in their mind), this is the place for you to spend money. Such men have traditionally spent freely and fast. Though some of them are gay, as we all know most are not. Remove those signs in an area where once they were prominent, and it's like reversing the signal: Now it means that men *with* attachments can spend their money here—which is often men with a great deal more money, men who want to spend it in business. That's really what old Chief McAdoo's comment was all about.

The Forty-second Street Development Project wants families to spend their money here. So the visible signs of sex have got to go. There might be a problem, however, McAdoo's principle notwithstanding. According to Timothy J. Gilfoyle, in an essay on the history of the Times Square area, "From Sourbrette Row to Show World: The Contested Sexualities of Times Square between 1880 and 1995,"

> in the two decades preceding the 1995 zoning restrictions, New York witnessed a decrease in the number of adult entertainment venues, many of them located in Times Square. In 1977, for example, 245 such enterprises— adult theaters, massage parlors, bookstores and peepshows—operated in the city. By 1993, the number had dropped more than a quarter to 177, barely greater than the level in 1976. In Times Square alone, adult stores decreased from 96 to 35 between 1977 and 1987.

Businesses are supposed to move in when vice is at its peak—not ten years after the wave has crested and is a decade into its ebb. What this may just sign is that those four planned office towers, if not the rest of the brave new mall, could suffer the fate of so many of the country's artificially built-up downtown areas over the last decade or two—Minneapolis, Minnesota; Springfield, Massachusetts—where no one wants to live or work, so that, as Jane Jacobs warned in her 1961 volume *The Death and Life of Great American Cities*, because there's not enough intertwined commercial and residential variety to create a vital and lively street life, the neighborhood becomes a glass and aluminum graveyard, on its way to a postmodern superslum, without even going through the process of overcrowding—abandoned before it's ever really used.

Across Eighth Avenue from Stella's, toward the corner of Forty-sixth Street, between the Eighth Avenue Grocery and the Lilipul Video Store, the Full Moon Saloon is a narrow bar on the ground floor of a five-story apartment house, most of whose upper windows have been cinder-blocked over. The blocks are painted the same taupe as the rest of the wall. With its yellow marquee like a grubby, overhead welcome mat, its door is set in the wall at a slant. Just inside, an ancient grill turns half a dozen hot dogs on its aluminum rollers. They go for fifty cents apiece—for those drinking. The bar counter runs from the front almost to the back, stopping only to make room for a jukebox with a yowling, twanging selection of country and western, and a pool table. The walls are close enough so that a variety of cut-down cues lean in the corner, along with a few full-sized ones for diagonal shots. Opposite the bar, attached to the wall, a plank bench painted black runs pretty much the length, where customers can drop their workbags, paper parcels, and knapsacks—or, sometimes, sit. (If this *were* a gay bar, that would be the meat rack.) On the back wall, larger than life, a comic book–style cowboy and cowgirl cavort across the doors to the tiny Men's and Ladies'.

The Full Moon is one of four diminutive dives, all within walking distance and managed by a guy named Ernie Schroeder. The other three are over on Ninth. Ruddy's, which he's recently converted into a jazz bar, is actually getting a some-what upscale clientele. The others are pretty much all working-class. Only one is officially a gay bar. (We'll visit that one later.)

Hoke Jones is the daytime bartender at the Full Moon. He works the morning shift, till noon, when a pair of barmaids take over for the more profitable afternoon and evening hours.

Hoke is a bit hard for me to write about.

Why?

I first met Hoke in the Capri in the late seventies. A head taller than anyone else in the balcony, in his jeans, denim jacket, and orange workboots, he filled the theater seat with his wide, bear-like body. On a small, cubical head, a walrus to rival Nietzsche's overhung a harelip whose surgical correction went on up through the first half-inch of the right nostril of a nose whose deformity had rendered it Negro-wide. Talk about hands? Hoke's are among the biggest I've ever seen. And he was an inveterate nail biter. His cock was notably shorter than mine, but generously uncut. Most foreskins have all the presence of a fold of parachute cloth over a grape. Hoke's, however, I can only call meaty.

Our half dozen encounters in the Capri in as many months were all but word-less. I assumed he was a laborer in from Brooklyn or Queens. Then one evening I

97

came into the old Fiesta to see him at the bar's end, talking to a bartender about an air conditioner that, sure, he'd be glad to help him install.

Within the week, when I was walking in the bright sunlight of Ninth Avenue, I saw Hoke in a grubby T-shirt with a Day-Glo orange traffic-alert vest strapped over it, carrying a tool chest through the gate around a street excavation where half a dozen other workmen hung out under a tent or climbed down into a hole in the paving. I stayed some moments to watch, till one of the workmen gave me a grin. I smiled back, then walked on.

Hoke was a city sewer worker.

We had a few more all but silent encounters at the Capri.

Over the next six weeks I saw him twice more at the bars, once on the subway, and several times more at his job. Once I saw him coming out of a little grocery store; another time I glimpsed him leaving a bar to hurry west (there's no public transportation in that direction)—and realized he probably lived not in an outlying borough but in the neighborhood. Then one day the excavation on Ninth was closed over, the orange metal gates were packed up, and the trucks were gone.

The hard part?

Well—

Hoke was one of those guys who, if I ran into him on the street and he'd simply said, "Hey, you—meet me tonight at six. I'm going to the mountains of Afghanistan, and I think it might be nice to have you along," abandoning family, friends, and all worldly possessions, I'd have been there at six, without a second thought.

He had that effect on me.

I'm wonderfully lucky in that I've known three such men. I'm also lucky that I've known *only* three. It may be some index of the condition itself when I mention that, until this writing, I was not aware—until I started tabulating aspects—that *two* of them had harelips, though never once, till this moment, have I consciously thought it a physical characteristic I was particularly taken with.

If you've felt that way about someone, then I don't need to tell you—about hanging out in a crowded bar for three hours, where I could just see the back of his head and one shoulder of his plaid flannel shirt, because being in the same space with him made me feel so . . . good; about hurrying faster and faster toward another street excavation, to realize, ten feet off from the blue and white van, it was all Con Ed workers and not the municipal crew at all; about walking from end to end of Forty-sixth Street twelve times in an afternoon, because I'd passed him there the day before and figured if I hung around long enough I might glimpse him there again; about staring down at manhole covers in the sidewalk for fifteen moody minutes, wondering if he were beneath one of them; about ambling along streets and hanging around corners where he even *possibly* had walked.

One evening—after Hoke had not been in the Capri for more than seven or eight months—I saw him at O'Neill's. Euphoric with the pleasure of being in the same room with him, all my clothes damp and my stomach weak from the terror of rejection, this time, clumsily but insistently, I started a conversation, and finally learned that his name was Hoke Jones. (Yeah, Jones.) "Hoke" was a childhood nickname for Howard that had stuck. Born in Brooklyn, he was Irish and German. Of course he only vaguely remembered me from the movies (or, as I thought of it, he'd forgotten that a half dozen of his orgasms were already incorporated into my bone and flesh). "Well, you know, I had a lot of different guys in there—and I was usually lookin' at the screen." Yes, a city sewer worker, Hoke had been married but was now divorced. He had two sons and three daughters, most of them all but grown. (My own daughter at the time was four.) He was friendly with his ex-wife much in the way I was with mine. A couple of years back he'd moved into an apartment house in the neighborhood.

And somehow I managed to blurt, "If I'm stumbling all over myself talking to you, it's because—well, you're the most attractive man I've . . . *ever* seen in my life!"

To which his response was to laugh, sit back on the bar stool, and, surprised, declare, "Who—*me?*"

Over thirty-five, most people with a certain sexual sophistication also have a certain sexual generosity. Hoke was not really looking for a relationship, he explained. But—it was his suggestion—if I really thought he was that hot, why didn't I visit him at his house?

We made a date: I was to come to his apartment the following Friday at seven o'clock. "It'll give me time to get cleaned up after I get off work."

When I rang the doorbell, he answered in a maroon bathrobe. A Joe Jones album was playing on his hi-fi. Jones was his favorite singer, he explained. (We laughed about the coincidence of the names.) He had an all but complete collection of everything Jones had ever released. I'd brought him some tiny, innocuous house present. "Oh," he exclaimed while opening it. "Hey! That's so *nice!*" Hoke's apartment had warm gray walls, on which hung a couple of pieces of abstract sculpture, one of which surrounded a clock.

He offered me a glass of wine.

We sat down, Hoke on the couch and me in an armchair, for some conversation.

I remember I asked him, "Why are you sitting on your hands?"

He laughed. "'Cause they're so big and ugly. And I bite my nails so bad. My mother used to make me sit on them, for an hour, every time she caught me chewing on them. It never broke me of the habit—it just got me in the habit of trying to hide them whenever I could."

"I think you have the most beautiful hands I've ever seen," I said. "They look like hands that have done something, put things together, taken them apart. You can look at them and see how they hold and heft their own histories—in a way that's . . . well, breathtakingly beautiful."

"These . . . ?" He pulled them out and looked at them. "You gotta be kiddin'."

"As far as I'm concerned," I told him, "movie stars should have hands that look like that. They'd be a lot more popular."

"Yeah?" Hoke laughed. "Name me a movie star who bites his nails."

"Brad Davis," I told him. Davis was then only a few years away from his fame in *Midnight Express*.

"He does?"

"Yes," I said. "And if you want some more heartthrobs, there's Andy Gibb and—"

"No. That's okay."

"—but their hands are nowhere near as big and as strong as yours, so you have them beat out by miles," I finished up.

Hoke said, "*Mmmm.*"

Because it made him uncomfortable, I changed the subject. And about ten minutes later, yes, we were in bed.

Forty minutes after *that*, with both of us laughing pretty hard—me in my underwear and on the couch and Hoke once more in his bathrobe, in the chair this time—Hoke offered the best analysis possible of what had been, alas, a three-quarter-hour sexual fiasco.

"I'm afraid," Hoke told me, "I'm just one of those great big clumsy guys with a little girl inside him who's dying to get out. The only problem is, *she's* basically a lesbian, so there's just not a whole lot in you she can relate to sexually. That's why we were both having all those problems." Now he laughed. "You like things about me I think are just *awful*! I mean, you actually *like* it that I still got my foreskin—while I don't think I could even *go* to bed with another man who wasn't circumcised."

"Since I am," I said, "you'd think we'd be compatible. But I suppose I see what you mean." Then I told him, "It's true, I'd hate to see it go. But if that's the way you feel about it, why don't you have yourself cut?"

"I'm scared—that it would hurt. Once I heard about a grown guy who did it and got all *sorts* of complications. Besides, my doctor says there's no reason to." He laughed again. And a little later, just before I left, Hoke said, "You know, maybe if we'd met when we were kids or something, you could've got me to like some of the things about me I just think are big and clumsy and ugly. I mean, they're all things I was born with. I ain't never gonna get rid of them. But I think it's a little late for making me change the way I feel about them now. The reason we couldn't make it is that I don't even *wanna* like the things about me that you think are just great! I mean, I probably don't need anybody who *hates* 'em. But for any kind of regular thing, I need a guy who just sort of ignores them, like I do—but wants to put that little girl through all her changes. I mean—what? You're thirty-six. I'm thirty-eight. What it is, see, is we're both homosexual. You need somebody the same sex as you. I need somebody the same sex as me. But that's just not each other."

I shook his hand. We said good-bye (and Hoke did not give me a hug). And I walked out the door—just about sixteen years ago. I've seen Hoke, now at one bar, now at another, maybe seven times since. Two of those times, perhaps, we've spoken. ("Hey, I don't see you in the movies any more, Hoke."

("Naw, I don't go in there now. They just don't do it for me any more.") The last of them, I was among a group of some seven or eight patrons at Stella's to whom, after mentioning he'd retired from the sewers some years back, Hoke announced he would be starting as the morning bartender at the Full Moon, Wednesdays through Saturdays. "Eight to noon—if you're around then, drop in and say hello."

So: What did Hoke think about the Times Square renovation?

At ten in the morning (a couple of days beyond my visit with Jimmy), only five or six guys sat at the Full Moon's bar. The piecemeal mirrors along the barback were covered with the yellowing Special Tax Stamp paper, photos of one of the afternoon barmaids' kids, and various notes and posters, one of which read, "All Bartenders: Joe Cox is not to be served in this bar. By order of Ernie."

As I came in, Hoke was leaning on the counter, on the phone, finishing a warm and obviously happy conversation, pretty clearly with one of his kids. "Okay, honey, I'll see you soon. I love you. Good-bye." The phone was all but hidden in his immense fist against his cheek. I greeted him, and he stood up, smiling, still tall, still massive in a pale blue zip-up leisure shirt. His iron-gray hair has a few white streaks. (Mine's gone all gray.) The mustache that so generously covered his harelip reconstruction is thinner. (And I wear an eight-inch white beard and, unlike Hoke, am fifty pounds heavier.) How long, now, had Hoke lived in the neighborhood?

"Twenty-two years. It's a nice neighborhood. I retired from city work three years ago in the summer of '93, 'cause the street diggin' job was just getting worse and worse. Since then, I've been doing off-shift bartender stuff for extra cash. Yeah, I still live in the same apartment on Ninth and Forty-sixth." What kind of bar is this? "The Full Moon? Well, it's not a gay bar—except that every bar in New York has *some* gay people in it. This is a working-class bar. 'Cause we're over here on Eighth Avenue, we got a few more drunks I guess than some of Ernie's other spots. But this is a place where working guys come when they get off work—or, yeah, a few of them, when they need a nip just before they go in." What did Hoke think of the changeover? "Well, they cleaned it up. Like Bryant Park. When the Javits Center came in, that knocked out a lot of stuff. But I think they got carried away. They took away lots of legitimate small places too. I mean the hot dog stands. The little stores. The rice and beans places. They did that for the money—believe me, not for their health. The real estate's all gone sky high. A lot of people who lived around here have moved to Jersey. Eventually it'll all work out—for the rich, anyway. But not for the average man. This has always been a neighborhood you could find anything you wanted in. Now you can find anything except a decently priced apartment. Just a moment—" and Hoke stepped from behind the bar to put some quarters in the jukebox. "There," he said, coming back just as Bonnie Raitt demanded, *Let's give 'em somethin' to talk about.* "That's better."

What did Hoke think about the suppression of the sex movies and peep shows, and about the rezoning?

"In one way it's good—but not in another. I thought they should just make them not display or advertise on the outside. Then they could have kept all that going, and it wouldn't have bothered anybody. I mean, you're never gonna *really* get rid of it. It'll just pop up somewhere else—in Brooklyn or Queens, if they don't let it go on in the city here." What about the relation of sex and drugs? "If you *make* them go together, sure, they'll walk along with one another, hand in hand. Just like sex and violence. But that's because you force them into the same places. They say they're going to put all the sex stuff on the river, but the girls who used to be walkin' around over there, half naked with their tits fallin' out, they're gone. You know—" here Hoke leaned a meaty forearm on the bar (I took a quiet breath)—"I remember back in the seventies, before Dinkins was mayor, before Koch even, when Abe Beame was just starting to run for office. He was down on Forty-second Street, giving a speech on the corner. I can see him now, pointing up at Show World. 'If you elect me, I promise you before my term of office is through, this place will be *gone* from the city!' That's *just* what he said!"

"Well, Beame is gone. Koch is gone. Dinkins is gone. And Giuliani is going to be gone soon. (I voted for him when he came in. But I *sure* wouldn't vote for him now.) And Show World's still there." Hoke chuckled.

Did Hoke have any objections to my using his real name?

"Well, maybe you should change— Naw, go on. Why not? Nobody's looking for me. I don't got no record or anything."

I said thanks for the talk. We shook hands, and I walked out onto Eighth Avenue.

I've mentioned that the man I've lived with happily now for getting on to six years also frequented the Capri. Did I mention, however, that he's also Irish and

German; and also from Brooklyn; and also has big hands (though not *quite* so big as Hoke's), and also bites his nails? (No harelip, however. Sigh.) Anyway, I'm just happy that, in the course of our talk, even sixteen years later, Hoke didn't think to ask me to go with him to Afghanistan. . . .

Behind the Port Authority, on a wedge cut off Forty-first Street at Ninth Avenue, a little darker than Stella's, a little raunchier, a little funkier, and a bit larger than the Full Moon, sits the Savoy—Ernie's gay bar. On the floor just inside the entrance, a few weeks back they inlaid a scroll reading: "For a Gay ol' Time . . ." Older customers tend to be white and black. Younger ones are black and Hispanic. When someone in his twenties comes in and greets a friend, often there's what I guess is a secret handshake. Of Masonic complexity, it involves a hug, taps on the chest, joined fingers, grappled fists, a sweep of the arm.

"This place started off as the Savoy Grill," explained Bill, an older white customer at the bar. (A moment before, after telling him about this piece, I'd asked him his profession. He gave me a look that said, "You must be crazy, asking me to reveal that in a place like this!" Obviously, though, he's a gregarious fellow who likes to talk.) "Used to have a hotplate counter, right along there. The guys from the post office and the Port used to come in. When it went gay, well . . . the owner decided to go where the bar had already gone. He changed the name to Hombres for a few years. Now it's the Savoy again." What did Bill think of the New Forty-second Street? "For gay men in this city, it's a disaster! The city says it'll rezone all the sex-specific businesses to the waterfront. Here, because there were so many other kinds of activity around, we were safe. The men who go over there looking for sex will be preyed on by muggers, bashers, not to mention all the legal forms of exploitation. Except for what's running around on the street, they've pried pretty much all the 'undesirables' out of the neighborhood. Our people are just assuming that, because the big cats have managed to swipe the money-making properties, when the porn houses and the peep shows open up on the river—each one at least five hundred feet from the next—the city'll look the other way and business can go on as usual. But because of the legal changes, the police can still nail anyone and any place they want to. That means, when they want to, they will!"

Wandering back to the corner of Forty-second and Eighth to catch the 104 bus home, at Ben's shoeshine stand I stopped again.

"My business? Actually, it's a little better: I don't have to keep chasing away the drug dealers. They were so thick on this corner, decent people were afraid to stop!" Ben looked across the street at Richard Basciano's Show World Center, which opened on Eighth Avenue just above Forty-second Street in 1977. "They should never have put that thing here. They should all be over at the river. They got four thousand guys a day goin' through that place. The girls who work there basically live off tips. Sure. Who's the landlord gonna rent to—somebody who can pay a couple of thousand a month, or a thousand bucks a day?" (Actually Show World

On the southwest corner of Forty-second Street and Eighth Avenue, two young men talk among the passersby. To the picture's far right, on the corner diagonally across, by the green knobs that indicate the subway entrance, directly below the Coca-Cola sign, the umbrella, out that day, shades Ben's shoeshine stand. Within the year, the buildings behind it with the gates down before their windows will also be torn down. The building across the street to the right of the picture's middle for some fifteen years housed a "Gay Strip Show and J/O Club" on the second floor. When, a year after this picture was taken in October 1996, the building was demolished, substantial pieces of its mirrors and mosaics clung to the brick wall for another year, till they too were pulled down, a glittering reminder of the young men who had worked there.

owns its own building—as well as, till a couple of years ago, most of the Strip's north face.) "But that's what's brought Times Square down!" With its fundamentally heterosexual business, Show World Center is one of the places that may escape the move—so there'll still be a little color left, a few memories of an older Forty-second Street.

I said good-bye and went to wait for my bus—a black gay man, in my mid-fifties, who's utilized the sexual outlets of this neighborhood for more than thirty years. What kind of leaps am I going to have to make now between the acceptable and the unacceptable, between the legal and the illegal, to continue having a satisfactory sex life?

As my bus came, behind me Ben called out to the woman in a passing couple: "*Mmmm*! Hey, *there*, sweetheart . . . !"

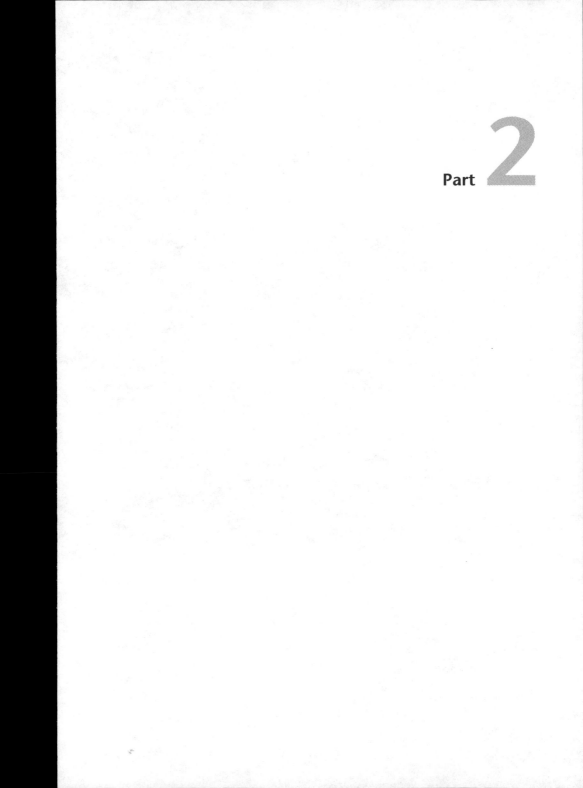

Part 2

... Three, Two, One, Contact: Times Square Red

December 1997–April 1998

As long as there is something like experience, it is not entirely mine.

—AVITAL RONELL, *Finitude's Score*

§0. The primary thesis underlying my several arguments here is that, given the mode of capitalism under which we live, life is at its most rewarding, productive, and pleasant when large numbers of people understand, appreciate, and seek out interclass contact and communication conducted in a mode of good will.

My secondary thesis is, however, that the class war raging constantly and often silently in the comparatively stabilized societies of the developed world, though it is at times as hard to detect as Freud's unconscious or the structure of discourse, perpetually works for the erosion of the social practices through which interclass communication takes place and of the institutions holding those practices stable, so that new institutions must always be conceived and set in place to take over the jobs of those that are battered again and again till they are destroyed.

My tertiary thesis, to which now and again we shall return, is that, while the establishment and utilization of those institutions always involve specific social practices, the

§A. Among other things, this essay is an attempt to explain what is going on in the following anecdote:

A group of friends entered a Soho gallery opening—some young painters and their acquaintances. At the group's center was a woman painter—we'll call her Jane Pharnim—who had a show up currently at a nearby gallery we'll call Quincunx.

As Jane and the group stood around talking and sipping from

plastic glasses of white wine, a man joined them, saying to Jane, "You're Jane Pharnim, aren't you? I saw your show just yesterday over at the Quincunx. I was very impressed. Probably, I shouldn't tell you this, but I'm going to be reviewing it for *Color and Form*. I don't think it'll be a problem though, since I was planning to give it a pretty good review anyway. But it's nice to get a chance to meet you and say hello. The only picture that somewhat puzzled me was that big gray and yellow one in the back. It seemed so different from all the others."

"It is, in many ways," replied Pharnim. "But in others—do you remember the little red one right beside the door . . . ?"

"One of my favorites—yes."

"Well, the big gray and yellow one has the identical structure, turned upside down and rotated left/right, as the little red one. I wanted to see if I could make it work like that, larger and with a cooler palette. That's why it's there with the others—even though, yeah, I know it doesn't *really* look like it belongs."

"Now, that's interesting. No, I didn't see that. I'll have to rethink that one before I hand in the review."

effects of my primary and secondary theses are regularly perceived at the level of discourse. Therefore, it is only by a constant renovation of the concept of discourse that society can maintain the most conscientious and informed field for both the establishment of such institutions and practices and, by extension, the necessary critique of those institutions and practices—a critique necessary if new institutions of any efficacy are to develop. At this level, in its largely stabilizing/destabilizing role, superstructure (and superstructure at its most oppositional) *can* impinge on infrastructure.

§1.1. We are all aware that landlords and tenants exist in a fundamentally antagonistic relationship. Generally speaking, throughout most of what we might call the middle classes of our society, landlords tend to be somewhat better off financially than their tenants. Certainly the class war is as strong there as between any groups save, perhaps, workers and employers.

With that in mind, here is a tale:

A black woman born in Nottaway, Virginia, my maternal grandmother came from Petersburg to New York City at age eighteen in 1898 and moved to Harlem in 1902, when it was still a German neighborhood. With my grandfather, an elevator operator in a down-

The conversation drifted on. Soon—and separately—both the reviewer and Pharnim left.

But the next morning one of the painters who had been part of the group (and who, unlike Pharnim, hadn't yet had a gallery show but would very much have liked one) explained to a friend, "You know, today in the art world it's all who you know, who you meet, who you network with. Last night, I was at an opening with Jane, when this art reviewer came over to talk to her. She practically dictated her review to him, word for word . . ."

Now, despite the young man's somewhat over-glib analysis, certain things *did* go on in the encounter at the art opening and certain things *did not.*

We can clarify some points right away: The encounter did not bring about the writing of the review. (The reviewer had been assigned the review before he met Pharnim.) The encounter did not change a bad review into a good one. (If the reviewer had already decided to write a bad one, it's unlikely he would have introduced himself—or at least would have avoided letting Pharnim know who he was.) Most obviously, the encounter did not acquire for Pharnim her show at the Quincunx.

town office building and later a Grand Central Terminal redcap, she took rooms in the first house in Harlem opened to blacks, on 132nd Street between Seventh and Lenox. Owned by a black man married to a white woman, the house rented to men and women working as servants in the neighborhood. My grandmother told of returning to her rooms after work, while the Germans sitting in front of their houses along Seventh Avenue played zithers through the evening.

A number of times in the sixties and seventies, Grandma spoke of the social practice in the twenties, thirties, and, in a few places, into the forties, of the landlord's annual or sometimes semiannual visit to her apartment. My sense is that these visits were notably different from the monthly visits *to* the landlord to pay the rent—in the days before universal banking.

Expected by both tenants and landlords, the visits allowed tenants to point out directly to the building's owner any breakages or repairs that were needed. The owner got a chance to see how the tenant was treating his or her property. By opening the door for less formal ones, these scheduled visits established an arena for social interchange. From them, landlords gained a sense of the tenants as individuals and tenants took a sense of the landlord as a person.

Taken out of context, however, what the young male artist, who lusts after just such a show himself (". . . today in the art world it's all who you know, who you meet, who you network with . . ."), could easily be taken to mean is that such encounters might well lead to such shows, such reviews.

Gallery openings and art gatherings are typical fields for networking. The exchange was typical of those that easily and often occur in networking venues. What *did* happen at the gallery opening was an exchange of specialized information about one somewhat problematic canvas in Pharnim's show—information that may or may not find its way into an already favorable review; and, yes, it is information that might not have been available to the reviewer had there been no networking venue to bring him, even so briefly, together with the artist.

By the end of this essay, I hope we shall have an even clearer idea not only of what went on and what did not go on in this networking situation, but also some understanding of what the young man who witnessed the encounter *thought* he was seeing and what he felt his stake was in drawing the conclusion that he did about the necessity of networking.

Yes, there might be a spate of cleaning in the apartment in the days before the landlord came. Certainly there might be a rush of painters and plumbers in that same month—so that during the visit itself everyone might come off at his or her best. But the visits meant that in those situations in which there were problems on either side that could be resolved only by the greater forces of the class war itself (an eviction, a suit against a landlord for a major dereliction of necessary repairs), there was nevertheless a social field in which either side could ask for leniency or at least understanding from the other; and often it could be granted. Similarly, either side could personally entreat the other to straighten up and fly right, and many times this was enough to avert any litigious confrontation.

In no way did the social practice obviate the socioeconomic antagonism between the *classes*. But it tended to stabilize relationships at the personal level and restrict conflict to the economic level itself—keeping it from spilling over into other, personal situations. What eroded this practice of landlord visits was, first, the economic forces of the Depression. Pressures on tenants (from the exhaustion of having two or three jobs to the anomie of having no job at all) became such that tenants began housing extra materials or extra people in their apartment to the point that a good day's cleaning could not cover over the evidence. Models for bourgeois living standards became less available, as did the time and the energy to implement them. Landlords found themselves unable to afford keeping the facilities in the first-class condition tenants expected.

Tenants began to see the visits as prying. Landlords began to see the visits as a formal responsibility empty of content and—finally—an unnecessary nuisance, in which they had to listen to demands they could not afford to meet. Repair work was now delegated to a superintendent whose job was to carry out those repairs as inexpensively as possible. While more stringent rules were instituted to restrict property-damaging wear and tear, in practice tenants were now allowed greater leeway in what they might do to the house. Older tenants saw the failure of the landlord to visit as a dereliction of responsibility. But younger tenants cited the "privilege" of better-off tenants in more lavish properties, often paying far higher rents, to forgo such visits. Why shouldn't the privilege of the better-off be a right—the right of privacy—for all?

§1.2. For the last twenty-one years, I have lived in a five-floor walk-up, rent-stabilized apartment at the corner of Amsterdam and Eighty-second Street. In that time, the owner of the building has *never* been through my apartment door. Once, in 1992, he shouted threats of legal action against me from the landing below—threats that came to nothing when, in retaliation, I hired a lawyer. This past February 1997, when what became a four-alarm fire broke out in the building at five in the morning, he visited his property for a brief half hour at seven-thirty A.M. Standing out on the street among the fire engines, he declared how grateful he was that no

§B. During tight times the landlord's visit facilitated a comparatively humane prioritizing of repairs—allowing tentant complaints to be looked at somewhat more holistically in terms of how much discomfort each involved. A loose window sash in the bathroom of a twenty-year-old student, spending weekends with his family and who is willing to wait till March to have it fixed is not necessarily the same complaint as a loose window sash of the bathroom of an seventy-year-old couple, more sensitive to cold and temperature change. A family with two working adult incomes may be amenable to the suggestion, "Have the window repaired at your own expense, give me the receipt, and I'll subtract half the cost of the repairs from this coming December's rent and the other half from January's, giving you a monetary break for the holidays."

By exploiting such prioritizing strategies the landlord could sometimes stabilize and smooth out his or her cash flow problems and the seasonal crunches that invariably fell to such a business.

Of course, such prioritizing could be abused—repairs might be put off indefinitely. It is as frustrating for tenants to have to ask for the same repair month after month as it is for landlords month after month to have to nag their tenants for the rent. In cases of landlord abuse, however, tenants sought refuge in a system in which a loose sash was a loose sash, no matter who had it. They wanted, as well, a time limit for when it would be fixed. Nevertheless, when a land-

one had been hurt; then—in his shako and (the only man in three decades I've ever seen wear one) fur-collared overcoat—he left. But those are the only two times I have seen him in person—or has he, I assume, seen me.

On the one hand, when repairs have been needed, and even more so after that brief shouting match in the hall, occasionally I've thought that the more personal relations my grandmother maintained with her landlord during the early decades of this century might well have made things go more easily. Were my landlord someone with whom, twice a year, I sat over a cup of coffee in my kitchen, I might have been able to negotiate speedier and better-quality repairs—repairs for which, often, I would have been willing to share the financial weight, repairs that would have benefited the property itself. And certainly we both might have bypassed the emotional strain of the aforementioned shouting match.

On the other hand, I try to imagine my landlord's response if he had visited during the first ten months after I had to collapse my Amherst apartment with my New York digs (when I was under precisely the same sort of socioeconomic pressures that had eroded away the practice of visits in the first place) and my apartment's back three rooms looked more like lord used prioritizing intelligently and responsibly, it could work as a social gift to everyone.

In the situation where a loose sash is a loose sash, to be fixed within a given time, general repair quality tends to be lower, with poorer-grade materials. Though the tenants benefit as a group, often as individuals they suffer more inconvenience. ("The repairman is coming at 10:00 A.M. on Tuesday. You'll just have to take a day off from work.")

The visit from the landlord recalls another sort of visit, the charity visit, which goes back at least (in England) to the 1840s, and continues to this day with the social worker's visit.

The particular aspect of the visits I am interested in, however, is when the visitor him- or herself has the money and the authority to instigate repairs and effect material changes. When a visitor functions *precisely as a mediator between* the tenant and whoever authorizes (and pays for) the changes, we have a situation that I will designate as the linear chain model. Such chains function largely to filter out the specific, social, idiosyncratic information that made prioritizing possible. Such chains—even of two or three people—become a major

an overfull Jersey warehouse space than a home with people living in it. What if he had come during the previous five years, when regularly I let friends use the place, two and three times a month, as an Upper West Side party space? (More than half a dozen years after the fact, I still meet people who tell me they have been to "great parties" at "my" house, when *I* wasn't in attendance.) During the same period, I let a succession of friends and acquaintances stay there during the 130-odd days a year I was in Amherst, teaching at the University of Massachusetts. Landlord visits would have curtailed such practices severely, though in neither case, on my side nor on his, was the *letter* of the law violated.

§1.3. At the rhetorical level, the trace of the social practice my decade-and-a-half dead grandmother spoke about still lingers in the language, as tenants on the Upper West Side speak about our landlords' "seeing to" certain repairs, even though the landlord will not and does not intend to set eyes on anything within the front door of the building—just as the term "landlord" is itself a rhetorical holdover from a time and set of social practices when the *important* things the owner was "lord" over were, indeed, "land" and the

mechanism to ensure not only that a loose sash is a loose sash, but that a broken pane, a loose sash, and a window frame pried out and shattered by an organized gang of apartment thieves are, all of them, just a "window repair." "tenants to the land," rather than the buildings erected upon it.

§1.4. The betraying signs that one discourse has displaced or transformed into another are often the smallest rhetorical shifts. A temporal moment (and a sociological location) in the transformation from a homosexual discourse to a gay discourse may be signaled by the appearance in the 1969 fall issues of the *Village Voice* of the locution "coming out to" one's (straight) friends, coworkers, and family (a verbal act directed toward straights) and its subsequent displacement of the demotic locution "coming out into" (gay) society—a metaphor for one's first major gay sexual act. Between the two locutions lie Stonewall and the post-Stonewall activities of the gay liberation movement. Equally such a sign might be seen to lie at another moment, at another location, in the changeover from "that's such a camp" to "that's camp." The intervening event there is Susan Sontag's 1964 *Partisan Review* essay, "Notes on Camp." I have written of how a shift in postal discourse may be signed by the rhetorical shift between "she would not receive his letters" and "she would not open his letter." What intervened here was the 1840 introduction of the postage stamp, which changed letter writing from an art and entertainment paid for by the receiver to a form of vanity publishing paid for by the sender. (There *was* no junk mail before 1840.) One might detect a shift in the discourse of literature by the changeover from "George is in literature" (when literature was a profession) to "George's library contains mostly history and literature" (when literature became a class of texts). The explosion of print in the 1880s, occasioned by the typewriter and the linotype, intervene. The shift from landlord visits to superintendents in charge of repairs is signaled by the rhetorical shift between "the landlord saw to the repairs" as a literal statement and "the landlord saw to the repairs" as a metaphor. I say "shifts," but these rhetorical pairings are much better looked at, on the level of discourse, as rhetorical collisions. The sign that a discursive collision has occurred is that the former meaning has been forgotten and the careless reader, not alert to the details of the changed social context, reads the older rhetorical figure as if it were the newer.

As are the space of the unconscious and the space of discourse, the space where the class war occurs as such is, in its pure form, imaginary—imaginary *not* in the Lacanian sense but rather in the mathematical sense. (In the Lacanian sense, those spaces are specifically Symbolic.) Imaginary numbers—those involved with *i*, the square root of minus-one—do not exist. But they have measurable and demonstrable effects on the real (i.e., political) materiality of science and technology. Similarly, the structures, conflicts, and displacements that occur in the unconscious, the class war, and the space of discourse are simply too useful to ignore in explaining what goes on in the world we live in, unto two men yelling in the hall, one a landlord and one a tenant, if not mayhem out on the streets themselves, or the visible changes in a neighborhood, like Times Square or, indeed, the Upper West Side, over a decade or so, and the specificities of rhetorical shift.

(Repeatedly Foucault described discourse, or at least a part of it, as "an" unconscious. In a 1968 interview ["Interview with Michel Foucault" (*Dits et écrits*, 654)] he said, "In a positive manner we can say that structuralism investigates an unconscious. It is the unconscious structure of language, of the literary work, and of knowledge that one is trying at this moment to illuminate." In his 1970 preface to the English edition of *Les Mots et les choses*, he wrote that his work intended to "bring to light a *positive unconscious* of knowledge: a level that eludes the consciousness of the scientist and yet is part of scientific discourse"; italics in original.)

Often, like many contemporary theorists, I have wondered whether the fundamental spaces of all three aren't one, as the death of God, the Author, and Man each has clarified another of the axes describing that space.

·   ·   ·

§1.5. Starting in 1985 for the first time, in the name of "safe sex," New York City began specifically to criminalize every individual sex act by name, from masturbation to vaginal intercourse, whether performed with a condom or not—a legal situation that has catastrophic ramifications we may not crawl out from under for a long, long time. This is a legal move that arguably puts gay liberation, for example, back to a point notably before Stonewall—and doesn't do much for heterosexual freedom either.

This is a rhetorical change that may well adhere to an extremely important discursive intervention in the legal contouring of social practices whose ramifications, depending on the development and the establishment of new social practices that promote communication between the classes (specifically sexual and sex-related), are hard to foresee in any detail.

§1.6. An important point: I do not think it is in any way nostalgic to say that under such a social practice as my grandmother knew, both landlord and tenant maintained better relations than I do with my landlord today. The practice of landlord visits was a social arena of communication, which, when utilized fully, meant that both landlord and tenant had to expend more time, energy, and money in order to maintain a generally higher standard of living for the tenant and a generally higher level of property upkeep, which restricted the abuse of that property for the landlord. On both tenant and landlord, greater restrictions obtained as to what was expected and what was not. The practice eroded when the money was no longer there, when the time and energy had to be turned, by both, to other things, and when practices formerly unacceptable to both had, now, to be accepted, so that the visits became a futile annoyance to both sides and were dropped.

But the establishment of, say, tenant associations—at which landlords are occasionally invited to speak and meet with their tenants—*begins* to fill the vacuum in the array of social practices that erosion leaves.

At the same time, they do not fill it in the same way.

The fact that such relations may have been more pleasant does not, however, mean that those relations were somehow more authentic than mine to Mr. Buchbinder. All that relative pleasantness suggests is a confirmation of my primary and secondary theses, which *are* about pleasure, after all—pleasure in its most generalized form (though pleasure no less important or social for that): the pleasant.

§1.7. A recapitulation.

Given the mode of capitalism under which we live, life is at its most rewarding, productive, and pleasant when large numbers of people understand, appreciate, and seek out interclass contact and communication conducted in a mode of good will.

The class war raging constantly and often silently in the comparatively stabilized societies of the developed world perpetually works for the erosion of the social practices through which interclass communication takes place and of the institutions holding those practices stable, so that new institutions must always be conceived and set in place to take over the jobs of those that are battered again and again till they are destroyed.

While the establishment and utilization of those institutions always involve social practices, the effects of my primary and secondary theses are regularly perceived at the level of discourse. Therefore, it is only by a constant renovation of the concept of discourse that society can maintain the most conscientious and informed field for both the establishment of such institutions and practices and, by extension, the necessary critique of those institutions and practices—a critique necessary if new institutions of any efficacy are to be established. At this level, in its largely stabilizing/destabilizing role, superstructure (and superstructure at its most oppositional) *can* impinge on infrastructure.

§1.8. So stated, these points appear harmless enough. Over the last decade and a half, however, a notion of safety has arisen, a notion that runs from safe sex (once it becomes anything more than making sure your partner uses a condom when you are anally penetrated by males of unknown HIV status, whether you are male or female) to safe neighborhoods, safe cities, and committed (i.e., safe) relationships, a notion that currently functions much the way the notion of "security" and "conformity" did in the fifties. As, in the name of "safety," society dismantles the various institutions that promote interclass communication, attempts to critique the way such institutions functioned in the past to promote their happier sides are often seen as, at best, nostalgia for an outmoded past and, at worst, a pernicious glorification of everything dangerous: unsafe sex, neighborhoods filled with undesirables (read "unsafe characters"), promiscuity, an attack on the family and the stable social structure, and dangerous, noncommitted, "unsafe" relationships—that is, psychologically "dangerous" relations, though the danger is rarely specified in any way other than to suggest its failure to conform to the ideal bourgeois marriage.

Such critiques are imperative, however, if we are ever to establish new institutions that will promote similar ends.

§2. The linear chain linkage into which the earlier practice of landlord visits with tenants might be said to have degenerated reminds us that the linear chain as an information conduit is a relatively artificial social form. Most social interchanges of information and material occur in various forms of social nets (as opposed to chains).

Generally speaking, in a net situation information comes from several directions and crosses various power boundaries, so that various processes—modulating, revisionary, additive, recursive, and corrective (all of them critical, each of them highlighting different aspects)—can compensate for the inevitable reductions that occur along the constitutive chains. Considered as information dispersal processes, nets are far more efficient than chains. Not all nets are, however, the same.

Social nets can be of more or less complexity, of greater or lesser density. When the net density is comparatively low, we find ourselves focusing on the contacts between individual net members and often ignoring the net-like structure in which the individual contacts occur. When the net density is high, we find ourselves more likely to focus on the overall network.

Starting from the above as the most arbitrary and provisional of observations, I will go on to discuss two modes of social net practice (and the discourses around them that allow them to be visible as such) that I designate as "contact" and "networking." Like all social practices they make/generate/create/sediment discourses, even as discourses create, individuate, and inform with value the material and social objects that facilitate and form the institutions that both support and contour these practices.

§2.1. Contact is the conversation that starts in the line at the grocery counter with the person behind you while the clerk is changing the paper roll in the cash register. It is the pleasantries exchanged with a neighbor who has brought her chair out to take some air on the stoop. It is the discussion that begins with the person next to you at a bar. It can be the conversation that starts with any number of semiofficials or service persons—mailman, policeman, librarian, store clerk or counter person. As well, it can be two men watching each other masturbating together in adjacent urinals of a public john—an encounter that, later, may or may not become a conversation. Very importantly, contact is also the intercourse—physical and conversational—that blooms in and as "casual sex" in public rest rooms, sex movies, public parks, singles bars, and sex clubs, on street corners with heavy hustling traffic, and in the adjoining motels or the apartments of one or another participant, from which nonsexual friendships and/or acquaintances lasting for decades or a lifetime may spring, not to mention the conversation of a john with a prostitute or hustler encountered on one or another street corner or in a bar—a relation that, a decade later, has devolved into a smile or a nod, even when (to quote Swinburne)

"You have forgotten my kisses, / And I have forgotten your name." Mostly, these contact encounters are merely pleasant chats, adding a voice to a face now and again encountered in the neighborhood. But I recall one such supermarket-line conversation with a woman who turned out to have done graduate work on the Russian poet Zinaida Hippius, just when I happened to be teaching Dmitri Merezhkovsky's Christ and Anti-Christ trilogy in a graduate seminar at the University of Massachusetts: Merezhkovsky was Hippius's husband, and I was able to get some interesting and pertinent information about the couple's wanderings in the early years of the century.

I have at least one straight male friend who on half a dozen occasions has gotten editorial jobs for women he first met and befriended while they were working as topless dancers in various strip clubs that put them on the fringe of the sex workers' service profession.

A young street hustler in the Forty-second Street area whom I knew (but was not a client of) introduced me to a new client of his once—a twenty-six-year-old lapsed Jesuit priest—for whom I shortly secured a job at a paperback publishing house, in much the same manner.

Another supermarket-line conversation was with a young man who was an aspiring director, looking for some science fiction stories to turn into brief teleplays. I was able to jot down for him a quick bibliography of young SF writers and short stories that he might pursue. Whether or not it came to anything, I have no way of knowing. But it was easy and fun.

Still another time, it was a young woman casting director who needed someone to play the small part of a fisherman in a film she was working on. She decided I would be perfect for it, and I found myself with a weekend acting job.

One Saturday morning in January '98, my vacuum cleaner shorted out and an hour later I set it on the street by the gate before the garbage cans for my building, after making a mental note to shop for a replacement that weekend. Forty minutes on, at my local copy center, I was getting a set of photocopies for an earlier draft of this very piece, when a broad-faced, gray-eyed Italian American in his late thirties, wearing a shiny red and blue jacket, wandered in: "Anyone wanna buy a wet-dry vacuum cleaner? Ten bucks." My first suspicion was that he was reselling the one I'd just abandoned. My second was that the one he was selling didn't work. A look disproved the first. Plugging his machine into an outlet in the shop's baseboard for a minute disproved the second. So I went home once more with a vacuum cleaner:

Contact.

Contact encounters so dramatic are rare—but real. The more ordinary sorts of contact yield *their* payoff in moments of crisis: When there is a fire in your building (of the sort I mentioned above), it may be the people who have been exchanging pleasantries with you for years who take you into their home for an hour or a day, or even overnight. Contact includes the good Samaritans at traffic accidents (the two women who picked me up and got me a cab when my cane gave way and I fell on the street, dislocating a finger), or even the neighbor who, when you've forgotten your keys at the office and are locked out of your apartment, invites you in for coffee and lets you use her phone to call a locksmith; or, as once happened to me in the mid-sixties when my then-neighborhood, the Lower East Side, was at its most neighborly and under the influence of the counterculture, a London guest arrived on Wednesday when I was out of town and expecting him on Thursday. Someone living across the street, who didn't know me at all, saw a stranger with two suitcases on my apartment stoop looking bewildered, invited him in to wait for me, then eventually put him up for a night until I returned.

A final example: My current lover of eight years and I first met when he was homeless and selling books from a blanket spread out on Seventy-second Street. Our two best friends for many years now are a male couple, one of whom I first met in an encounter, perhaps a decade ago, at the back of the now closed-down Variety Photoplays Movie Theater on Third Avenue just below Fourteenth Street. Outside my family, these are among the two most rewarding relationships I have: both began as cross-class contacts in a public space.

Visitors to New York might be surprised that such occurrences are central to my vision of the city at its healthiest.

Lifetime residents won't be.

Watching the metamorphosis of such vigil and concern into considered and helpful action is what gives one a faithful and loving attitude toward one's neighborhood, one's city, one's nation, the world.

I have taken "contact," both term and concept, from Jane Jacobs's instructive 1961 study, *The Death and Life of Great American Cities*. Jacobs describes contact as a fundamentally urban phenomenon and finds it necessary for everything from neighborhood safety to a general sense of social well-being. She sees it supported by a strong sense of private and public in a field of socioeconomic diversity that mixes living spaces with a variety of commercial spaces, which in turn must provide a variety of human services if contact is to function in a pleasant and rewarding manner. Jacobs mentions neither casual sex nor public sexual relations as part of contact—presumably because she was writing at a time when such things were not talked of or analyzed as elements contributing to an overall pleasurable social fabric. Today we can.

When social forces menace the distinction between private and public, people are most likely to start distrusting contact relations. In *The Death and Life of Great American Cities* (98–111), Jacobs analyzes how limited socioeconomic resources in the area around a public park (lack of restaurants, bathrooms, drugstores, and small shops) can make the mothers who use the playground and live near it feel that their privacy within their home is threatened—thus markedly changing their public attitude to interclass contact. Briefly, a park with no public eating spaces, restaurants, or small item shopping on its borders forces mothers who live adjacent to it and who thus use it the most to "share everything or nothing" in terms of offering facilities of bathroom use and the occasional cup of coffee to other mothers and their children who use the park but do not live so near. Because the local mothers feel they must offer these favors to whomever they are even civil with (since such services are not publicly available), they soon become extremely choosy and cliquish about whom they will even speak to. The feel of the park becomes exclusive and snobbish—and uncomfortable (and inconvenient) for mothers who, in carriage, dress, race, or class, do not fit a rigid social pattern.

Similarly, if *every* sexual encounter involves bringing someone back to your house, the general sexual activity in a city becomes anxiety-filled, class-bound, and choosy. This is precisely *why* public rest rooms, peep shows, sex movies, bars with grope rooms, and parks with enough greenery are necessary for a relaxed and friendly sexual atmosphere in a democratic metropolis.

Jacobs's analysis stops short of contact as a specifically stabilizing practice in interclass relations. She dismisses "pervert parks" as necessarily social blights (largely understandable in the pre-Stonewall 1950s when she was collecting material for her book, but nevertheless unfortunate), though she *was* ready to acknowledge the positive roles winos and destitute alcoholics played in stabilizing the quality of neighborhood life at a *higher* level than the neighborhood would maintain without them.

I would recommend her analysis, though I would add that, like so much American thinking on the left, it lacks not so much a class analysis as an *interclass* analysis.[1]

Eventually we shall touch on—though we shall by no means exhaust—the topic of the menace of violence in some of these urban venues.

·   ·   ·

1. Astute as her analysis is, Jacobs still confuses contact with community. Urban contact is often at its most spectacularly beneficial when it occurs between members of *different* communities. That is why I maintain that interclass contact is even more important than intraclass contact.

§2.2. Here is one of my favorite contact stories told me by a friend:

"I run annually in the Boston Marathon. I'm not a first-class runner, and my goal is to finish in the top hundred—last year I came in at 117th place—but I train regularly. Every morning for the first half of the year I take a ten-mile run. Then, as the marathon gets closer, I up it to twelve, fifteen, then twenty miles. One morning in March I was just starting my run across the Brooklyn Bridge, when I heard some woman scream. I looked around, and this fifteen- or sixteen-year-old kid had just snatched her pocketbook and was taking off. I called, 'Stay here, ma'am, I'll get that back for you,' turned around, and took off after him.

"It was a really interesting feeling, knowing as I ran after that kid that there was no way, unless he'd been in training for a marathon three years himself, he was going to outrun me. I stayed about five yards behind him. We were running around street corners there in the Heights. I didn't think he was going to make a full ten minutes, but he lasted for almost thirteen or fourteen. Finally when he was leaning against a wall, falling down on one knee, I went up to him, took the pocketbook out of his hand, gave him a slap on the back of his head, and said, 'Okay, now don't *do* that again!' Then I took off back to the bridge. It was almost twenty minutes later, and the woman was gone by then. But there was some identification in the pocketbook. I called her up and took it over to her that evening. She's a very interesting woman . . ."

Rare, heroic, and certainly not to be counted on, such contact nevertheless represents one of the gifts the human variety of the city can bestow.

§3.0. There is, of course, another way to meet people. It is called *networking*. Networking is what people have to do when those with like interests live too far apart to be thrown together in public spaces through chance and propinquity. Networking is what people in small towns have to do to establish any complex cultural life today.

But contemporary *networking* is notably different from *contact.*

At first one is tempted to set contact and networking in opposition. Networking tends to be professional and motive-driven. Contact tends to be more broadly social and appears random. Networking crosses class lines only in the most vigilant manner. Contact regularly crosses class lines in those public spaces in which interclass encounters are at their most frequent. Networking is heavily dependent on institutions to promote the necessary propinquity (gyms, parties, twelve-step programs, conferences, reading groups, singing groups, social gatherings, workshops, tourist groups, and classes), where those with the requisite social skills can maneuver. Contact is associated with public space and the architecture and commerce that depend on and promote it. Thus contact is often an outdoor sport; networking tends to occur indoors.

The opposition between contact and networking may be provisionally useful for locating those elements between the two that do, indeed, contrast. But we must not let that opposition sediment onto some absolute, transcendent, or ontological level that it cannot command. If we do, we will simply be constructing another opposition that we cannot work with at any analytical level of sophistication until it has been deconstructed—a project to which we shall return.

§3.1. The benefits of networking are real and can look—especially from the outside—quite glamorous. But I believe that, today, such benefits are fundamentally misunderstood. More and more people are depending on networking to provide benefits that are far more likely to occur in contact situations, and that networking is specifically prevented from providing for a variety of reasons. Put up with me while I talk a bit about the particular networking institution with which personally I am most familiar, the writers' conference—though I hope you will be able to generalize my points to all sorts of gatherings, conferences, interest groups, conventions . . . and art openings.

•   •   •

§3.2. To most young writers the writers' conference represents a social field where, each hopes, one of three things will occur: (1) s/he will be discovered (by some nebulously defined power group) because of his or her extraordinary talent; (2) s/he will be able to bring her- or himself, by some "heroic" extraliterary act, to the attention of someone perceived as powerful, an established writer or editor; or (3) because of social proximity someone in a position of power (writer, editor) may take a liking to him or her and proffer some unspecified favor that will improve the young writer's lot. Certainly other desires are present as well—the desire for sociality among one's equals, in the field of desire that we mark with the terms "ambition" and "opportunity." But, I submit, those others are, if only because they cannot be officially articulated, the shared form of inner, expectant concern.

Indeed, the prizes to be won at such an affair look extraordinary—at least at first. A well-known writer befriended there might eventually write a blurb for your novel or introduce you to his friends, moving you onto a new social level. The editor encountered over drinks might say, "Sure, *send* me your manuscript," and thus launch an entire writing career. The writer on your own level, befriended there, may favorably review your first novel, if and when it is eventually completed, accepted, and published. Looking at the reality of the situation, however, we have to ask: How many times do any of these things actually happen? The answer is: Precisely enough times to stabilize the notion of such conferences in the minds of a general aspiring writer population—and not a lot more.

The stated and articulated reason to attend the conference is, of course, to learn what will be taught about the practice of writing itself, its aesthetics and its business. But it is the rare writer who attends a writing conference without, at least from time to time, some fantasy about one or all of the primary three happening. For just that reason, the conference will appear to be that much *more* exciting at precisely the points where something on that order appears to occur, so that the folklore about such occurrences, when they do happen, answers the secret desires we bring with us and often provides our major picture of the event.

I want to discuss all three of our opening possibilities in terms of anecdotes from my experience of writers' conferences since I attended my first, thirty-seven years ago.

§3.21. In July 1960, when I was eighteen, I received a work scholarship (I had to wait tables for the summer) to the Bread Loaf Writers' Conference at Middlebury College in Vermont. The scholarship was arranged by a Harcourt Brace editor who had read one of my early novels.

Although I did not know it at the time, writers' conferences often develop "stars" among the attendant writers—one or a few aspiring writers who, for one reason or another, are singled out ("discovered") and, for the duration of the conference, are the envy of the other participants. They are the people or person on whom all the good things and tangible benefits of the conference appear to heap themselves, one after the other.

On the second day at Bread Loaf, to my surprise, I became such a "star." It was a discovery of precisely the sort I and, indeed, thousands of fledgling writers have dreamed about at thousands of writers' conferences, before and since.

Among the three-hundred-odd attendees at Bread Loaf that year, I had submitted a novel for the novel writing workshop. (There were some thirty people in the workshop, who met in a country style meeting house.) William Sloan, of the publishing house William Sloan Associates, began the opening session by saying that, after looking over all thirty-odd submissions in the novel category, the only one that "seemed to have any novelistic life whatsoever" was one that he was going to read a passage from. From my seat in the third row, I heard him begin to read out a section from the third "chapter" of my "novel":[2] Visiting a community center where a black band has just finished rehearsing, a young white man

2. Actually, as has been practically every MFA thesis I've encountered in the past decade, my "novel" was a series of loosely connected stories with some common characters—and equally uninteresting.

sits at an unused set of drums to begin playing an impassioned jazz percussion improvisation.

When Mr. Sloan finished reading (he read it *very* well), he made the point from the podium that such writing could only come from someone who loved this sort of music. Then he asked if the author were in the room and could confirm this.

Sheepishly I stood up and confessed that, actually, I disliked jazz as a musical form. My father had an extensive jazz collection, however, and for a brief while (two or three weeks) had played cornet with Cab Calloway's band back in the early days of the Cotton Club. Yes, I had heard jazz all my life; for better or worse, I knew a fair amount about it. With one or two exceptions, however, I found it really distasteful—and the character who played it so well in my novel was a psychotically manipulative young white fellow, the villain of the piece, who subsequently maneuvered one after the other of the main black characters to their doom.

Immediately, Mr. Sloan revised his statement: Such writing, then, could only come from *strong feeling*, one way or the other. People laughed. Things proceeded.

But from having been singled out at the conference on the first day, soon I was being invited to the professional parties with the faculty. I remember several of the young writers around me telling me, "You've got it made."

Once Bread Loaf was over, a woman editor at Random House who had attended the conference, and had once worked with Sloan, invited me to lunch. She also read my novel and told me, at that lunch, pretty much what half a dozen editors had told me before the conference, when I had been submitting the book here and there. "You write well, but the basic subject matter is just not what makes a commercial novel." Today I would add the following to her articulate advice: To deal with the type of material I was dealing with (young people, mostly juvenile delinquents) would require a much more linear structure than I was using. Had I been able to organize that material into a more linear "adventure" form, rather than a mosaic of anecdotes, character sketches, and impressions (imagine as much of the plot as I've already discussed presented in the manner of *The Notebooks of Malte Laurids Brigge*), I would have had a substantially better chance of placing my book. In short, while the conference responded to the talent I showed, once the conference was over, the realities of publishing, in the form of the Random House editor who had kindly befriended me there, fell into place. And to the extent that the book represented a literary experiment (and, in my own mind, it did), the fact is, it was not a strong enough experiment to win over any of the dozen-odd commercial editors who, over the two years before (and in the year afterward), read it.

My Bread Loaf and Bread Loaf–connected experiences doubtless made it easier for me to talk to the editors at Ace Books, who, a year and a half later, oversaw the publication of my first novel—an entirely new book that I had not even thought about writing back in Vermont. But when, in June 1962, Ace Books accepted that new novel for publication, *none* of the social contacts either with editors or with the half dozen other "big-name writers," e.g., Robert Frost, John Ciardi, John Frederic Nyms (then editor of *Poetry*), or that year's Pulitzer Prize winner, Allen Drury, whom I had met at Bread Loaf—at which I had "starred" and been, indeed, "discovered"—were even tangentially entailed, directly or indirectly, with my actual breaking into print.

§3.22. A second anecdote addresses that second desire, the "heroic" extraliterary act. A dozen years after Bread Loaf, at a writing workshop in Michigan, *I* was now the (relatively) well-known writer, called upon to lead a group of some twenty younger writers. One particularly determined young man in his late twenties (happily married and a father of two) had his leg in a cast for the duration of the conference. He had written a story that, indeed, I felt was fairly good—certainly putting him in the top fifth of the talent quotient as I judged it. His view of what was to be gained by networking was, however, sadly inflated. One night, cast and all, he climbed through my window—and into my bed! (Later, I learned that this had begun as a somewhat inebriated dare among the students, when he had declared to them that he would "fuck anything" and they had immediately picked me out as the . . . *ahem*, impossible object of desire.) Our postcoital conversation lasted till dawn. Its result was that, since I thought he had talent as well as moxie, once the conference was over I told him he could use my name and send his story to a couple of editors whom I knew. Neither editor bought it. Moreover, though I have remained a desultory and distant friend of the young man, he wrote no new work. After those two submissions, he became discouraged with his story and stopped sending it out.

The fact is, the kind of energy and imagination it takes to crawl through a window and, however "heroically" (read the import of the quotation marks as you wish), bed your instructor is very different from the kind of imaginative energy it takes to write and craft a succession of stories and novels.

For those who are interested, despite this single case of a bold and vigorous young man, over the thirty years I have taught at that particular writers' conference, I have recommended many more women writers to editors than I have young male writers—for no other reason than that I found more talented women writers in attendance at such conferences than men: two from *that* particular session. Those recommendations *also* did nothing.

§3.23. My third anecdote addresses the third hope of those who attend writers' conferences: Through proximity and general good will (i.e., non-"heroic" reasons), someone in a position of power will do something nice for you—though, in this case, it is not a tale from my own experience, but one from science fiction's history (possibly apocryphal), and one that many young writers have been aware of, as they have gone off to one SF convention or another. In the science fiction field, the story of how, back in the early 1950s, Ray Bradbury first came to the attention of readers beyond the boundaries of the science fiction "ghetto" (as it has been called) is a regularly rehearsed bit of SF folklore.

Having been published the year before, Bradbury's second hardcover collection of stories, *The Martian Chronicles* (1951), was on a remainder table in Brentano's Bookstore, then on Eighth Street in Greenwich Village. In the bookstore to buy up a few of the volumes, the thirty-two-year-old Bradbury struck up a conversation with a man standing next to him. Bradbury pointed out that, at the time, newspapers and literary magazines ignored *all* SF books that came in, leaving them unread, giving them, at best, a "Books Received" mention. His volume had gotten almost no reviews in the course of its shelf life.

Bradbury was articulate enough that the man—who turned out to be the writer Christopher Isherwood—was struck by his argument. A few issues on, in the *Saturday Review of Literature*, Isherwood (a regular reviewer for the magazine, who happened to have some say in what books he covered—a rare situation) took it upon himself to review Bradbury's book of poetic SF stories, so unlike the usual pulp fare of the day—and review it more or less favorably. In the same review Isherwood also mentioned the situation that Bradbury had outlined. The review and the position it adopted became somewhat notorious, and, as the first SF writer to be reviewed in the *Saturday Review of Literature* (and the last for *quite* a while!), Bradbury's career moved to a new level, from which it has never really retreated.

Though many attendees at writers' conferences arrive with such models of writerly generosity in mind, for a complex of material reasons this is precisely the sort of thing that is, however, *not* likely to happen in a networking situation such as a writers' conference.

The first thing to realize in the rehearsal of such a mythic tale is that, in *all* its elements—the chance meeting in a bookstore, the happenstance conversation with a stranger over the remainder table—quintessentially it's a tale of contact, *not* networking. As well, the contact brought about the *reviewing* of a book already in print, not the *publication* of one still in manuscript—as most of the attendees at writing conferences are hoping for.

At writers' conferences, what *is* likely to happen?

There might be a panel presentation on the difficulties or impossibilities of science fiction securing good review venues. Such a panel might mean that, instead of the review venue problem flickering as a vague and passing notion in the minds of one or three writers specifically faced with the problem, for the next few months an entire population of writers and readers will be particularly aware of the problem (and also particularly aware of the forces keeping the problem in place). Thus, if a chance to break through it arises (either through contact or something more institutionally begun), that chance will occur in a field that has been primed to a greater awareness of, if not sympathy for, the problem. (*That* is the benefit of networking.) Unfortunately today, unclear on the difference between the results each mode fosters, many people go into networking situations expecting or hoping for the extreme benefits of contact.

§3.3. With these three anecdotes in mind, we can now look at why so few stars are discovered at writing conferences (and why, when they are, it usually does them little direct good), why the "heroic" (i.e., extraliterary) attempt to bring oneself to the attention of the "powerful" at a writers' conference results in so little, and why simple acts of friendship are unlikely to produce major changes in career or reputation when they occur at a writers' conference—and, by extension, when they occur in any general networking situation.

The reason the networking situation is not likely to produce the sometimes considerable rewards that can result from contact situations is that the *amount* of need present in the networking situation is too high for the comparatively few individuals in a position to supply the much needed boons and favors *to distribute them in any equitable manner.* At the pleasant and chatty cash bar reception closing out the first day of panels and workshops at the writers' conference, it may *look* like a friendly and sociable gathering. At precisely the socioeconomic level (Symbolic, if you will) where the class war occurs, however, you have a situation analogous to a crowd of seventy-five or a hundred beggars pressed around a train station in some underdeveloped colonial protectorate, while a handful of bourgeois tourists make their way through, hoping to find a taxi to take them off to the hotel before they are set upon and torn to pieces.

Because of the way the networking situation is initially structured, the competition for favors (at the class war level), and even rewards of merit, is too great for them to be dispensed in anything like a fair and efficient manner—efficient to the people in need, fair as those in power judge it. The structure of desire that holds, as it were, the conference stable (quite a separate thing from the epistemological rewards that structure empowers and impels through its internal social organization) cannot be fulfilled by the conference—or the conferences themselves would simply erode.

The professed structure of the writers' conference is that of an epistemological dispensary. But the structure of desire beneath it that actually holds it stable and facilitates whatever dispersion of knowledge that takes place is that of a lottery with a very small chance of winning.

Just as with the social practice described by my grandmother of tenant and landlord at the table over coffee, the social practices and friendly interchanges that not only appear to, but *do,* fill the writers' conference reception halls, work to stabilize, retard, and mitigate the forces of the class war. In no way, however, can they halt or resolve that war. At best they allow that war to proceed in a more humane manner that keeps "war" merely a metaphor. In such situations, stabilization militates for *less* change in the power relations at the infrastructural level than might happen in a less concentrated and less competitive situation, even while existing social relations, happenstance, and yes, sometimes even merit might appear to be producing the odd "star" or lucky social "winner."

§3.4. Having said all the above, let me say that I attend writers' conferences regularly, and science fiction conventions (science fiction is one of my particular

writing interests) even more so. The clear and explicable reasons for my attendance are networking's epistemological benefits. Those benefits result from the
particularly dense field produced by the networking situation in which knowledge—not social favors—moves with particular speed. (The desire for social
favor *is* the fuel—or the form—that propels that information through the social
field.) At both formal sessions and informal gatherings, I find out about new
writers and interesting books, as well as new publishing programs and changes
in the business, much more quickly than I would without their benefits. By the
same token, people find out about what I'm doing and get a clearer picture of
my work. Because I'm comparatively comfortable appearing in public and discussing a range of topics from behind a podium or a panel table, people can get
a taste of the sort of analysis I do and can decide whether or not they want to
pursue these thoughts in my nonfiction critical work. Since I am a formal academic critic as well as a fiction writer—and a fiction writer who works in several
genres—this is particularly important and promotes among a small group of
concerned readers, at least, a more informed sense of my enterprise.

I feel that my career benefits regularly from the results of my networking. My
ultimate take on networking is, however, this: No single event in the course of my
career that I can cite has been directly *caused by* networking. Nevertheless, the results of networking have regularly smoothed, stabilized, and supported my career
and made it more pleasant (there is that term again) than it would have been without it.

In general I would say (and I would say this to young writers particularly):
Rarely if ever can networking *make* a writing career when no career is to be made.
It can make being a beginning writer more pleasant; it can make being a relatively
established writer more pleasant. But little or nothing will happen there that will
impel you from one state to the other. If anything, in the manner of stabilizing institutions, the social mechanics of conferences are more likely to retard career tran-
sitions, especially if you lean on them too heavily.

Basically the thing to remember is this:

One does not get publications by appearing in public.

One gets further invitations to appear in public.

Networking produces more opportunities to network—and that's about all.

Foucault gave us an analysis of power/knowledge. Desire/knowledge is just as important to understand—and, possibly and provisionally, in the current climate, even more so. Networking situations are self-replicating structures of knowledge and desire. Desire is what holds them stable and replicates them, and the absence on which that desire is based is the paucity of socio-material benefits everyone who attends them hopes to receive. The writer will get the most from the available networking situations if he or she attends them with a clear sense of this.

§4.1. Briefly, what makes networking different from contact is that, in networking situations, the fundamentally competitive relationship between the people gathered in the networking group is far higher than it is in the general population among which contact occurs.

The competition may be only barely perceptible at any given moment (or, under the camaraderie and good will of the occasion, all but invisible—it *is* the class war). Like the overriding economic forces of the class war and its effects on the individuals whose lives are caught up in and radically changed by it, the competition is seldom experienced *as* a force. It is pervasive nevertheless. Because of that competition in the networking situation, the social price tag on the exchange of favors and friendly gestures is much higher than it is in contact situations.

The people in line with you at the grocery counter are rarely *competing* with you for the items on the shelves in the way that young writers are competing for the comparatively rare number of publishing slots for first novels that can, under the best of conditions, appear each year. (Department store sales, however . . .) Even fewer in the grocery line will be competing for your specialized knowledge of the life of Zinaida Hippius. And they are not—at the moment—in competitive relations at all for the favors (whether of data or material help) that the established writer might be able to offer.

§4.2. Two orders of social force are always at work. One set is centripetal and works to hold a given class stable. Another set is centrifugal and works to break a given class apart.

The first set runs from identity, through familiarity, to lethargy, to fear of difference—all of which work to hold a class together. These are the forces that the networking situation must appeal to, requisition, and exploit.

The second set has to do, however, with the needs and desires that define the class in the first place: hunger, sex, ambition in any one of a dozen directions—spatial to economic to aesthetic to intellectual. These forces militate for breaking up a class, driving it apart, and sending individuals off into other class arenas. This is the level where, in a democracy, contact functions as an anti-entropic method for changing various individuals' material class groundings. The reason these forces work the way they do is simply that when such desires and needs concentrate at too great a density in too small a social space over too long a time, they become that much harder to fulfill—even when you pay generous honoraria

§C. The same principle which makes contact more likely to cede major material, social, or psychological prizes than networking makes interclass/intercommunity contact more likely to cede such prizes than intraclass or intracommunity contact: At the interclass and intercommunity level, competition for those prizes is likely to be less than it would be within a class, within a community.

to people who might help fill them, to move briefly into that crowded social space and dispense data about the process, without dispensing the actual rewards and benefits that those involved in the process seek. Love/desire/awe/fear/discomfort/terror/abjection (horror) *is* the human response range to greater or lesser power differentials.

The centripetal forces work to tame the components of that response.

Those components underlie and *are* the centrifugal forces.

§4.3. Recently when I outlined the differences between contact and networking to a friend, he came back with the following examples: "Contact is Jimmy Stewart; networking is Tom Cruise. Contact is complex carbohydrates; networking is simple sugar. Contact is Zen; networking is Scientology. Contact can effect changes at the infrastructural level; networking effects changes at the super-structural level."

Amusing as these examples are, it's important to speak about the very solid benefits of both forms of sociality. Otherwise we risk falling into some dualistic schema, with wonderful, free-form, authentic, Dionysian contact on the one side, and terrible, calculating, inauthentic, Apollonian networking on the other. Such would be sad and absurd. The way to do this is not to install the two concepts in our minds as some sort of equal, objective, and unquestioned pair of opposites. Rather, we must analyze both, so that we can see that elements in each have clear and definite hierarchical relations with elements in the other, as well as other elements that are shared. Only this sort of vigilant approach will produce a clear idea of what to expect (and not to expect) from one and the other, as well as some clear knowledge of why we should not try to displace one *with* the other and ask one to fulfill the other's job.

§D. Contact is random only in the sense that diversity represents a web of random needs vis-à-vis the constraints on the needs of all the members of a single profession, a single class.

In terms of the Bradbury tale, for example, Greenwich Village in the fifties was a neighborhood in which the chances of two writers running into one another at a bookstore remainder table were far higher than they would have been, say, three miles away across the river in a supermarket in Queens.

The same could be said of the Upper West Side, where I managed to snag the information about Zinaida Hippius or, indeed, the Variety Photoplays Theater, between the East and West Village, where I met my long-term social friends (and, a decade before, another long-term lover).

Were we so naive as to assert that in networking situations *there were* selection procedures while in contact situations *there were none*, we would only be rushing to set up those false and invalid oppositions.

Contact may be, by comparison, "random" (but doesn't one move to or from a particular neighborhood as part of a desire to be among—or to avoid—certain types of people, whether that neighborhood be Greenwich Village, Bensonhurst, or Beverly Hills?). And while networking may be, by comparison, "planned" (yet how many times do we return from the professional conference unable, a month later, to remember having met anyone of particular interest or not having retained any useful idea?), it is clear that contact is contoured, if not organized, by earlier decisions, desires, commercial interests, zoning laws, and immigration patterns. The differences seem to be rather matters of scale (the looser streets of the neighborhood versus the more condensed hotel or conference center spaces) and the granularity that allows others to dilute the social density with a range of contrasting needs and desires, as well as differences in social skills and, yes, institutional access.

§4.4. Contact is likely to be at its most useful when it is cross-class contact. Bradbury and Isherwood were, arguably, in the same profession, that is, both were writers. But they were also clearly at different class levels: beginning genre writer and established literary writer.

§4.5. Two modes of social practice: I call them contact and networking. They designate two discourses that, over the range of society, collide with and displace each other, reestablish themselves in new or old landscapes, where, at the level of verbal interaction, they deposit their rhetorical traces . . .

.   .   .

§4.6. Looking through the most recent nineteenth-century novel that I've been teaching, Flaubert's *L'Education sentimentale* (1869), I notice that two of the most important relationships to the protagonist, Frédéric Moreau, are definitely contact relationships. First and foremost is his relation with Monsieur and Madame Arnoux: he is attracted to Madame Arnoux as she sits on the deck of a steam ferry leaving Paris for the countryside along the Seine. The meeting is impelled wholly by desire, and Frédéric must put out a good deal of energy to make the contact occur and stabilize it as a social friendship across class boundaries (provincial bourgeois youth/urban sophisticate adults). His second cross-class contact friendship is with the young, good-hearted worker Dussardier, whom he meets in a street demonstration when he and a bohemian friend, Hussonet, also just met, decide all but arbitrarily to rescue the young worker from the clutches of the police. Both these relationships will develop elements of the tragic: Frédéric's inability to possess Madame Arnoux causes him a pain that pervades and contaminates every subsequent love relationship of his life. And Frédéric uses and abuses Dussardier in a positively shameful manner. Frédéric will eventually tell his upper-class fiancée that Dussardier has committed a twelve-thousand-franc theft (a lie that Frédéric tells as an excuse to borrow a like amount again to bail out M. Arnoux's family) that, because the young man is working-class, no one else will think to question. But when one compares *these* relationships to two that Frédéric has gotten through networking, they come off pretty well. Compare them with his relationship to Madame Dambreuse, the fantastically avaricious and vicious widow whom Frédéric barely escapes marrying: Frédéric knows her because he is given a letter of introduction by M. Rocque to her husband, the business tycoon M. Dambreuse— pure networking. The other distinctly networking relation is Frédéric's deeply vexing friendship with Sénécal, the mathematician who believes in a purely scientific politics—to whom Frédéric is first sent by his school friend Charles Deslauriers. In short, his networking ends up aligning him with extremely— even lethally—vicious men and women. Frédéric's fiancée-through-networking,

Madame Dambreuse, delights in the destruction of the social standing of his love-object-through-contact, Madame Arnoux, when the Arnoux's personal belongings are sold at auction. At the story's end, Frédéric's networking friend Sénécal runs his contact friend Dussardier through with a sword during a police encounter. Confronted with Madame Dambreuse's viciousness, Frédéric escapes her (she also, it turns out, has been done out of her fortune by the dead hand of her husband; Flaubert cannot pass up the irony). But Frédéric's own ability to love has been sadly and permanently impaired. Nevertheless, because it plays out identically with both a man *and* a woman, it's hard to avoid the suggestion that the antipathy between friends or lovers acquired by networking and those acquired by contact may well have been an intended part of Flaubert's complex allegory. Indeed, when one surveys the range of the great nineteenth-century social novels, from *Illusions perdues* (1837–43) and *Les Misérables* (1862) to *Great Expectations* (1860–61), many, though they do not name the contrasting modes, nevertheless present dramatic evaluations of the benefits and costs of the two modes of sociality. They even have sharp comments to make on what happens when one or another character relies too heavily on relationships that begin in one or the other mode.

§5.1. The current transformation of Times Square is a Baron Haussmann–like event. But like Haussmann's rebuilding of Paris, this event is comprised of many smaller events, among them the destruction of acres of achitecture, numberless commercial and living spaces, and, so far, the permanent obliteration of over two dozen theater venues, with (as of May 1997) more than a half dozen other theater demolitions planned within the next three months. With it all dies a complex of social practices, many of which turned on contact, affecting over any year hundreds of thousands of men and women, many of them native to New York City, many of them visitors. Further material developments alone will determine, say, whether the change in the legal status of specific sex acts that has legally preceded them (but, in the class war, only accompanies them) will or will not generate the rhetorical collisions that finally litter what already shows many signs of marking a major shift in the discourse of sexuality, straight and gay, as we respond to changes in the architecture, commerce, and quality of life in New York City.

§5.2. On March 10, 1997, the Buell Architecture Center sponsored a conference on Times Square's renovation, "Times Square: Global, Local," held at Columbia University and organized by Marshal Blonsky. The keynote speaker was Marshal Berman. The general sense I received (though it would be stunningly incorrect to call it a consensus) extended from, on the one hand, the view that, outside the general difficulties involved in going ahead with the project, there was no problem at all because the developers and architects were supremely sensitive to the needs of the city and its populace (a position put forward by spokesperson architect Robert Stern) to, on the other hand, an only slightly less sanguine view (put forward by Berman) that, if there *was* a problem, since there was nothing we could do about it anyway, we might as well go along with what was happening, smiling and supportive.

§5.21. In a revised version of his Buell Center talk, "Signs of the Times: The Lure of Times Square," which appeared in the Fall '97 issue of *Dissent*, Berman claims that I (along with Rem Koolhaas and the photographer Langdon Clay) am nostalgic for what he terms "the pre-AIDS golden age of hustling" (78).

If there was any such "golden age," I never had any experience of it, nor was I aware of any such thing at the time. (I assume he must mean pre-1982, possibly pre-'84.) The only thing I can think that lies behind Berman's misunderstanding is the erroneous assumption that all or most of the homosexual contact around Times Square was commercial, that is, involved hustlers or other sex workers. But the whole point is that, while the lure of hustlers most certainly helped attract the sexually available and sexually curious to the area, a good 80 or 85 percent of the gay sexual contacts that occurred there (to make what is admittedly a totally informal guess) were *not* commercial.

I do not want to demonize the profession of sex worker *per se;* but, as a material social practice that can be carried on in many ways and at many levels, the sex work that occurred there in many of its aspects can certainly be criticized—or, indeed, praised. And the relation of commercial sex to noncommercial sex was intricate and intimate.

What I regret personally is, however, the dissolution of that 80 percent where my own sexual activity and that of many other gay men were largely focused—though I am quite sure that others, both gay and straight, do miss equally the commercial side. The two orders of sexual relationship sat by one another in the sex movie theaters, drank shoulder to shoulder in the same bars, walked down the same streets, and lingered by the same shop windows to make themselves available for conversation in the afternoons and evenings. Though the relation between commercial and noncommercial sex was not without its hostilities (occasionally intense), in such a situation there is a far greater interpenetration of the two modes than in other areas—due to contact.

Because of the Forty-second Street area, my personal life as a New Yorker was a lot more pleasant from, say, 1980 to 1992 than it has been, after a three-year transition period, from 1995 to now. What made it more pleasant was the cheap films and the variety of street contact available—the vast majority of *that*, let me make it clear (so that I do not appear more of a

§E. If, as I say, 80 to 85 percent of the (gay) sexual encounters in the Times Square neighborhood were noncommercial, why does hustling so dominate the fictional accounts of the area's sexual machinery? (John Rechy's *City of Night,* Paul Rogers's *Saul's Book,* and Bruce Benderson's *User* are three excellent examples.) I can offer three reasons.

First, fictive rhetoric tends to reproduce its own form. The assumption—certainly stemming from fiction—that all sex, gay or straight, generated in the Times Square area was commercial is rather like the assumption of readers who, from a brush with novels by Anne and Charlotte Brontë (and possibly *Mary Poppins*), assume that thousands of poor but honest young women worked as live-in govern-esses in early-nineteenth century London (surely under two hundred)—while in *The Other Victorians* (1974) Steven Marcus says that, in the same years, the number of *prostitutes* in the city was estimated at various times as six thousand, as eighty thousand, and even higher. (What makes such tabulations all but impossible, as Marcus also notes, citing William Acton's study

of 1862, *Prostitution, Considered in Its Moral, Social, and Sanitary Aspects*, is that, male or female, prostitution is rarely a lifetime's profession, but may be pursued as a livelihood for an afternoon, a few months, or a handful of years.) But we generalize from our fictions.

Second, if only because of its economic motivation, hustling work is relatively more stable (the same men, *working* in the sex professions, are likely to show up on their beats day in and day out over a given period) and thus is more visible than even the frequent visitor availing himself of the hustlers' services, or the movies and/or peep shows for the noncommercial sex, three or four times a week. A man may show up two, three, or even

roué than I am) was *not* sexual at all; though, of course, much of it was. (And of those sexual contacts, in my case less than 10 percent were with hustlers. It's *not* my favorite sexual outlet. With no intention of sounding holier than any particular thou, one resorted to hustlers [and, in my case, not with much enthusiasm] when the noncommercial population seeking sex had been largely driven from the neighborhood. As I tell my classes regularly when I come out to them, my sexual ideal today tends to be substantially over forty. But many of the most pleasant nonsexual encounters would not have occurred if so many of the people there had not been open to sexual contact.) But it is not nostalgia to ask questions such as the ones that inform the larger purpose of this meditation.

How did what was there inform the quality of life for the rest of the city?

How will what is there now inform that quality of life?

Can anything of use be learned from answering such questions?

five times a week for a spontaneous jack-off session in a public rest
room taking a few minutes, or drop
in for anywhere between a few
minutes and a few hours or more
at one of the sex movies. These
would be among the committed
habitués of the noncommercial—
and still far less visible than the
hustler. And many more noncommercial utilizers of the neighborhood are there only once a week,
once a month, or once every six
months—and thus even more difficult to chronicle. The hustlers will
linger, however, around a given
street corner or in a particular bar
five or six hours a day, four to six
days a week. What will appear more
consistent is not the far more nu-
merous—but fleeting—noncommercial encounters, but the more consistent presence of the hustlers.
Thus, because it is more easily observed and researched, hustling is
more frequently written about.

Third, the line between the commercial and the noncommercial is
itself highly permeable and often
not easily fixed. By general consensus, a hustler is someone who
sets a price beforehand and, if the
payment is not agreed to, no encounter takes place.

But what of the poor to homeless man in the back orchestra of

．　　　．　　　．

§6.1. Four great office towers are currently in various stages of construction at the cardinal points of the New Times Square. As I write this (January 30, 1998), one, still lacking its curtain walls, is rising over the square above the blue board fences as a complex of girders. The demolition for a second has been completed. Two are still in the planning stages. Major construction is going on and has been going on for years now up and down Eighth Avenue from Forty-second Street to Fifty-second.

The Times Square problem I perceive entails the economic "redevelopment" of a highly diversified neighborhood with working-class residences and small human services (groceries, drugstores, liquor stores, dry cleaners, diners, and specialty shops ranging from electronics stores and tourist shops to theatrical memorabilia and comic book stores, interlarding a series of theaters, film and stage, rehearsal spaces, retailers of theatrical equipment, from lights to makeup, inexpensive hotels, furnished rooms, and restaurants at every level, as well as bars and the sexually oriented businesses that, in one form or another, have thrived in the neighborhood since the 1880s) into what will soon be a ring of upper-middle-class luxury apartments around a ring of tourist hotels clustering the sex movie who, after the sexual act is satisfactorily completed, asks, "Say, you wouldn't happen to have a couple of bucks on you—so I can go out, get something to eat, and get back in here to catch some sleep?"—who may, indeed, be as easily told, "Sorry, I don't have any money with me," as "Oh, sure. Here." Is that commercial?

What of the encounter that starts off particularly well, so that one person pauses and says, "Hey, I'm going to go out and get some sandwiches and a couple of cans of beer. I'll be back in ten minutes. What kind of sandwich you want? This way we can make an afternoon of it," and is told, "Great, man. Bring me a ham and cheese on rye with mustard." Is *that* commercial?

Finally, what about the man who, before the incident, presents himself as hustling, asking (however) for only five dollars, but who, when you shrug and say, "Sorry. I'm not paying," waits ten, silent seconds, then responds, "Ah, *fuck* . . . we'll do it anyway. Besides, I did it with you before. I know you're good." Is *this* commercial?

These, and numberless other scenarios the longtime visitor to the area can recount (the laborer from Queens who, after sex, in-

about a series of theaters and restaurants, in the center of which a large mall and a cluster of office towers are slowly but inexorably coming into being.

§6.2. The generally erroneous assumption about how new buildings make money is something like this: A big company acquires the land, clears it for construction, and commences to build. After three to five years, when it is complete, the company rents the building out. If the building is a success, all the offices (or apartments, as the case may be) are leased, and the site is a popular one, then and only then does the corporation that owns the building begin to see profits on its earlier outlays and investments. Thus the ultimate success of the building as a habitation is pivotal to the building's future economic success.

If this were the way new office buildings were actually built, however, few would even be considered, much less actually begun.

Here is an only somewhat simplified picture of how the process *actually* works. Simplified though it is, it gives a much better idea of what goes on and how money is made. A large corporation decides to build a building. It acquires some land. Now it sets up an extremely small ownership corporation, which is tied to

149

sisted on giving *me* fifteen dollars, because he "only went with hustlers" and would have felt uncomfortable if I didn't take *some* money from him; so, after five minutes of polite protest, I obliged), trouble the line between the commercial and the noncommercial encounter. Because the reality of the situation is intricate and often difficult to articulate—and because an overall fictional model preexists that is simpler and generally accepted; and because the whole situation lies outside the boundaries of the "socially accepted" anyway—often it's easier to let the extant rhetoric hold unchallenged sway. The result is an image of who is and who isn't a hustler that is as hard to pin down overall as who is and who isn't a whore—a concept which runs, as we all know, from the agented call girl to the woman who simply enjoys sex with several partners over a period of time.

the parent corporation by a lot of very complicated contracts—but is a different and autonomous corporation nevertheless. That ownership corporation, tiny as it might be, is now ready to build the building. The parent corporation also sets up a much larger construction corporation, which hires diggers, subcontracts construction companies, and generally oversees the building proper.

The little ownership corporation now borrows a lot of money from a bank—enough to pay the construction corporation for constructing the building proper. The small ownership corporation also sells stock to investors— enough to pay back the bank loan. The tiny ownership corporation (an office, a secretary, and a few officers that oversee things) proceeds to pay the parent construction corporation with the bank funds to build the building. It uses the stock funds to pay back the bank. Figured in the cost of the building is a healthy margin of profits for the construction corporation—and for the large corporation that got the whole project started—while the investors pay off the bank, so that *it* doesn't get twisted out of shape. Meanwhile both the ownership corporation and the construction corporation pay the parent corporation as their controlling stockholder.

Yes, if the building turns out to be a stunningly popular address, then (remember all those contracts?) profits will be substantially greater than otherwise. But millions and millions of dollars of profits will be made by the parent corporation just from the construction of the building alone, even if no single space in it is ever rented out. (Movies are made in the same manner, which is why so many awful ones hit the screen. By the time they are released, the producers have long since taken the money and, as it were, run.) Believing in the myth of profit only in return for investments, public investors will swallow the actual cost of the building's eventual failure—if it fails—while the ownership corporation is reduced in size to nothing or next to nothing: an office in the building on which no rent is paid, a secretary and/or an answering machine, and a nominal head (with another major job somewhere else) on minimal salary who comes in once a month to check in . . . if that.

§6.3. Two facts should now be apparent.

First fact: The Forty-second Street Development Project (I use this as a metonym for the hidden corporate web behind it) *wants* to build those buildings. Renting them out is secondary, even if the failure to rent them is a major catastrophe for the city, turning the area into a glass and aluminum graveyard.

A truth of high finance tends to get away from even the moderately well-off investor (the successful doctor or lawyer, say, bringing in two to four hundred thousand a year), though this truth is, indeed, what makes capitalism: In short-term speculative business ventures of (to choose an arbitrary cutoff point) more than three million dollars, such as a building or civic center, (second fact) the profits to be made from dividing the money up and moving it around over the one to six years during which that money must be spent easily offset any losses from the possible failure of the enterprise itself as a speculative endeavor, once it's completed.

The interest on a million dollars at 6.5 percent is about 250 dollars a *day*; on a good conservative portfolio it will be 400 dollars a day. The interest on ten million dollars is ten times that. Thus the interest on ten million dollars is almost a million and a half a year. The Forty-second Street Development Project is determined to build those buildings. The question is: How long will it take to convince investors to swallow the uselessness of the project?

Far more important than whether the buildings can be rented out is whether *investors think the buildings can be rented out.* In the late seventies, three of those towers were tabled for ten years. The ostensible purpose for that ten-year delay was to give economic forces a chance to shift and business a chance to rally to the area. The real reason, however, was simply the hope that people would forget the arguments against the project, so clear in so many people's minds at the time. Indeed, the crushing arguments against the whole project from the mid-seventies were, by the mid-eighties, largely forgotten; this forgetting has allowed the project to take its opening steps over the last ten years. The current ten-year delay means that public relations corporations have been given another decade to make the American investing public forget the facts of the matter and convince that same public that the Times Square project is a sound one. It gambles on the possibility that, ten years from now, the economic situations might be better—at which point the developers will go ahead with those towers, towers which, Stern has told us, *will* be built.

Berman's article in *Dissent*, which I referred to above, concludes with a postscript:

It begins, "I have just read in the *Times* of August 1 [1997], about a deal in the works to bring Reuters to Times Square. It wants to build an 800,000-square-foot office tower on Seventh Avenue and 42nd St." He goes on to say that Reuters is an interesting company (as if it would have anything more to do with the building than, perhaps, rent some 10 percent or less of its space) and he seems appalled that the awful Philip Johnson architecture planned over a decade ago will be utilized for the construction—as if, for a moment, *anyone* in a position of power involved in the deal cared. (Millions were paid for it; it must be used.) He concludes by suggesting that people who care about the Square raise the roof before the deal gets done.

Consider my roof raised.

. . .

§7.1. At the Buell conference a young sociologist countered my suggestion that there were some serious losses involved in the renovation process with the countersuggestion that at least the New Times Square would be safer for women.

§7.11. Which brings me to a survey of three topics—topics I will look at as systems of social practices related by contact: crime and violence on the street, the public sex practices that have been attacked and so summarily wiped out of the Times Square area, and the general safety of the neighborhood—along with the problem of safety for women.

First, the street-level public sex that the area was famous for, the sex movies, the peep show activities, the street corner hustlers and hustling bar activity were overwhelmingly a matter of contact.

Call-boy and call-girl networks, not to mention the various forms of phone sex, follow much more closely the "networking" model. But what *I* see lurking behind the positive foregrounding of "family values" (along with, in the name of such values, the violent suppression of urban social structures, economic, social, and sexual) is a wholly provincial and absolutely small-town terror of cross-class contact.

§7.12. A salient stabilizing factor that has helped create the psychological smoke screen behind which developers of Times Square and of every other underpopulated urban center in the country have been able to pursue their machinations in spite of public good and private desire is the small-town fear of urban violence. Since the tourist to the big city is seen as someone *from* a small town, the promotion of tourism is a matter of promoting the image of the world—and of the city—that the small town holds.

Jane Jacobs has analyzed how street crimes proliferate in the city. Briefly, lack of street-level business and habitation diversity produces lack of human traffic, lack of contact, and a lack of those eyes on the street joined in the particularly intricate self-policing web Jacobs claims is our greatest protection against street-level urban barbarism. Many people have seen Jacobs as saying merely that the *number* of eyes on the street do the actual policing. But a careful reading of her arguments shows that these "eyes" must belong to individuals with very specific and intricate social relations both of stability and investment in what we might call the quality of street life. Too high a proportion of strangers to indigenes, too high a turnover of regular population, and the process breaks down. Such proportions and such turnovers produce the dangerous neighborhoods: the housing project, the park with not enough stores and eating spaces bordering on it, the blocks and blocks of apartment residences without any ameliorating human services.

§7.13. Many non-city residents still do not realize that their beloved small towns are, per capita, far more violent places than any big city. New York has an annual rate of one murder per 108,000 inhabitants. Some large cities have as few as one per 300,000.

In 1967, however, I spent the winter months in a Pennsylvania town, which had a cold-weather population of under six hundred. That winter the town saw five violent deaths, homicides or manslaughters.

If New York City had five murders per six *hundred* inhabitants per winter, it would be rampant chaos! The point, of course, is that the *structure* of violence in cities is different from the structure of violence in small towns. Three of those small-town violent deaths, with their perpetrators and victims, occurred within two families who had a history of violence in the town going back for three generations—along with a rate of alcoholism truly epic. A social profile of those families would not be much different from the stereotyped pictures of the Hatfields and the McCoys of early sociological fame. The other two violent deaths that winter came when three adolescent boys from comparatively "good" families, bored out of their gourds during two solid weeks of snow, on a February evening's adventure pushed a car over a cliff. In the car a young couple was necking. The two young people died—but they were from another small town twenty-five or thirty miles away. Strangers, not residents. That particular incident produced an ugly and finally very sad court trial. One of the boys was sent to reform school. The other two got off with strong reprimands. But the town's general sense was that the victims shouldn't have been there in the first place. You stay in your own locality. Shut them in too long by the snow like that with nothing to do, and boys will be boys . . .

In a small town the majority of the violence that occurs (say, three out of five cases) does not really surprise anyone. People know where it's going to occur and in which social units (i.e., which two families) 60 percent of it will happen. They know how to stay out of its way. Your biggest protection from the rest of it is that you're *not* a stranger to the place; and you should probably stay out of places where you are. Comparatively speaking, the violence in a big city is random. No one knows where it's going to fall, who the next mugging victim, house-breaking victim, rape victim, not to mention victim of an apartment fire or traffic accident, will be.

Small towns control their violence by rigorously controlling—and often all but forbidding—interclass contact, except in carefully structured work situations. The boys of good families who killed the young couple (people in the town would be appalled that today I describe the incident in such words, though few of them would argue with me that that's what happened) did not associate with the sons and daughters of the local Hatfields/McCoys. When small towns are beautified and developed, their development generally proceeds in ways that make easier the location, unofficial segregation, and separation of the classes.

§7.14. Because our new city developments, such as Times Square, are conceived largely as attractions for incoming tourists, they are being designed to look safe *to* the tourist, even if the social and architectural organization laid down to appeal to them is demonstrably inappropriate for large cities and promotes precisely the sort of isolation, inhumanity, and violence that everyone abhors.

155

Traditionally cities keep their violence rate monumentally lower than in small towns by the self-policing practices that come from "eyes on the street," *supported by a rich system of relatively random benefits and rewards that encourage pleasant sociality based largely on contact.* That system of random rewards results in everything from basic intra-neighborhood "pleasantness" to heroic neighborly assistance in times of catastrophe. But in between these two extremes and even more important, in a society that prides itself on the widespread existence of opportunity, interclass contacts are the site and origin of a good many of what can later be seen as life opportunities, or at least the site of many elements that make the seizing of such opportunities easier and more profitable.

§7.15. The small-town way to enjoy a big city is to arrive there with your family, your friends, your school group, your church group, or—if you are really brave—your tour group, with whom you associate (these are all preselected network groups) and have fun, as you sample the food and culture and see the monuments and architecture. But the one thing you do not do is go out in the street alone and meet people. The fear of such an activity in New York City is, for most out-of-towners, one with the fear of bodily contagion from AIDS coupled with the equally bodily fear of hurt and loss of property.

Around 1990, I was returning to New York from a reading in Boston, on a plane with the Russian poet Andrei Voznesensky. Voznesensky was staying at the Harvard Club, just a block or two north of Grand Central Station, and he had been unaware that one could take a bus directly there from the airport rather than a taxi and save considerably.

When we got off at Grand Central, I suggested that he might want to use the facilities at the station. Very worriedly, he told me, "Oh, no. I don't think we better do that."

Naively, I asked, "Why not?"

"Because," he said, leaning close, "I don't want to catch AIDS."

Used to dealing with people who were afraid of touching people with AIDS or eating after them, I was nevertheless so surprised that someone might think he was at risk for contagion from using a public urinal that I was nonplussed. We parted less than five minutes later, and I have not seen him since.

But rather than take this as a spectacular example of misinformation and/or information, I think it is more interesting to see it as a cross-section of the process by which AIDS functions, on an international level, as a discursive tool to keep visitors to the city away from all public facilities and places where, yes, one might, if so inclined, engage in or be subject to any sort of interclass contact.

§7.16. Paradoxically, the specifically gay sexual outlets—the sex movies that encouraged masturbation and fellatio in the audience, the rougher hustler bars, the particular street corners that had parades of active hustlers—are or were often locales where the violence that occurs is closer to the high small-town level than to the overall lower big-city level. But, only to complete our paradox, that violence tends to be structured *like* small-town violence. If you frequent the place, quickly you learn from where and/or from whom it is going to come. A stranger or first-time visitor is probably far more vulnerable to that violence than a longtime, frequent habitué of the facility: the hustler bar, the sex theater, or the lowlife street corner. Someone who visits any one of these places from two or three times a week to monthly is likely to be pretty clear on which person—or, prejudicial as it sounds, which kind of person—will likely be the source of violence. That is why prostitutes can work the streets and neighborhoods they do. That is why, gay and straight, so many middle-class and working-class men feel perfectly safe visiting such urban spaces on a regular basis, often several times a week over years, even when, from statistics or just their own observation, they know perfectly well that every couple of weeks to every month—in extreme cases two or three times a day—some sort of robbery or fight or even bodily injury is done to a customer. In such places, however, the violence is *not* random. It follows more or less clear patterns that are fairly easily learned. Thus habitués feel—and, indeed, usually are—as safe as most people in any other small-town-*structured* violent environment. And, of course—the one thing Jacobs's analysis leaves out—during the times of nonviolence, which are *still* in the majority, in such locations the same principles of traffic, social diversity, and self-policing hold, yes, even here.

Another point that people lose track of: Public sex situations are not Dionysian and uncontrolled but are rather some of the most highly socialized and conventionalized behavior human beings can take part in.

§7.2. The sexual activity in the Times Square area (and by that I mean both commercial and noncommercial) has been hugely decried, called awful and appalling by many, including architect Robert Stern. We do *not* want a red-light district there, is the general cry of planners and organizers. People who utilized or worked in it, however, are sometimes a bit more analytical than those blanket dismissals. A good deal of what made the situation awful, when it was awful, was not the sex work *per se* but the illegal drug traffic that accompanied it, that worked its way all through it, and that, from time to time, controlled much of it. The mid-eighties saw an explosion of drug activity, focusing particularly around crack, that produced some of the most astonishing and appalling human behavior I personally have ever seen. Its extent, form, and general human face have yet to be chronicled.

In 1987 I had a conversation with an eighteen-year-old Dominican, who was indeed hustling on the strip. He was worried because he was living with a seventeen-year-old friend—another young crackhead—in a project further uptown.

The younger boy had been regularly selling all the furniture in the apartment, and, when his mother had objected, he had killed her.

Her body, the other boy told me, was still in the closet. The older boy did not know what to do.

I suggested that he tell his younger friend—whom I did not know and had not met—to go to the police.

Some days later, when I ran into the older boy, he told me that is indeed what his friend had done. The older boy I had talked to was now homeless.

One would have to be a moral imbecile to be in any way nostalgic for this situation.

Indeed, the major change in the area over the period between 1984 and 1987 was that professional prostitutes and hustlers—women generally averaging between, say, twenty-three and forty-five, and men somewhat younger, asking (the women among them) thirty-five to seventy-five dollars per encounter (and the men ten or fifteen dollars less)—were driven out of the area by a new breed of "five-dollar whore" or "hustler," often fifteen- , sixteen- , and seventeen-year-old girls and boys who would go into a doorway and do *anything* with anyone for the four to eight dollars needed for the next bottle of crack. Some of that situation is reflected in the scream that ends Spike Lee's film *Jungle Fever*.

It was that appalling.

It was that scary.

I hope we can look even on that period of human atrocity, however, with a clear enough vision to see (as was evident to anyone who walked through the neighborhood during those years, who lingered and spoke to and developed any concern for any of these youngsters) that this activity clotted in the area, that it grew and spread from there to other neighborhoods, that it reached such appalling dimensions as *a direct result* of the economic attack on the neighborhood by the developers, Robert Stern's employers, in their attempt to destroy the place as a vital and self-policing site, as a necessary prelude to their sanitized site.

The old Times Square and Forty-second Street was an entertainment area catering largely to the working classes who lived in the city. The middle class and/or tourists were invited to come along and watch or participate if that, indeed, was their thing.

The New Times Square is envisioned as predominantly a middle-class area for entertainment, to which the working classes are welcome to come along, observe, and take part in, if they can pay and are willing to blend in.

What controls the success (or failure) of this change are the changes in the city population itself—and changes in the working- (and middle-) class self-image. Sociologists will have to look at this aspect and analyze what is actually going on.

§7.31. Here I return to the question of Times Square as a space safe for women—which some, looking at the new development, have somehow managed to see it as. The first thing one must note is that there have always been women in Times Square, on Forty-second Street, and on its appendage running up and down Eighth Avenue. They were barmaids. They were waitresses. They were store clerks. They were ticket takers. I do not know how many women worked in the twenty-three-story Candler office building on the south side at 220 Forty-second Street between the former site of the Harris and the Liberty theaters, but for many years I regularly visited a friend who worked at a translation bureau run by a Mrs. Cavanaugh on the nineteenth floor. I will hazard that a minimum 40 percent of the workers there were women. Also, women *lived* in the neighborhood. Until the end of the seventies it was a place where young theater hopefuls—more men, yes, than women; but women nevertheless—lived in a range of inexpensive apartments and furnished rooms that extended over toward Hell's Kitchen (renamed, somewhat more antiseptically, Clinton a few years back). The vast majority of these women are not there now. And the developers see themselves as driving out (the minuscule proportion of) those women who were actual sex workers.

It is naive to think that these developers, who make a city space safe for one class of women by actively driving out another class, have any concern for women *as* a class. The Times Square developers' concern for women and women's safety extends no further than seeing women as replaceable nodes with a certain amount of money to spend in a male-dominated economic system.

Some of what was in the old Times Square worked. Some didn't work. Often what did—about, say, the sexual activity (and, despite the horror of the planners, much of it did: we have too many testimonies to that effect by both the customers *and* the sex workers)—worked by accident. It was not planned. But this does not mean it was not caused, analyzable, and (thus) instructive.

§7.32. The New Times Square is simply not about making the area safe for women. It is not about supporting theater and the arts. It is not about promoting economic growth in the city. It is not about reducing the level of AIDS or even about driving out perversion (i.e., noncommercial sexual encounters between those of the same sex who can find each other more easily in a neighborhood with sex movies, peep show activities, and commercial sex), nor is it about reducing commercial sex, hustling and prostitution.

The New Times Square is about developers doing as much demolition and renovation as possible in the neighborhood, and as much construction work as they possibly can. Some old-fashioned Marxism might be useful here: Infrastructure determines superstructure—not the other way around. And for all their stabilizing or destabilizing potential, discourse and rhetoric are superstructural phenomena.

There is, of course, a corollary particularly important for late-consumer media-dominated capitalism that's largely overlooked in classical Marxism: "Superstructure stabilizes infrastructure."

Briefly and more dramatically, superstructural forces (personal relations, the quality of life in the neighborhood) may decide a small business to shut down and vacate to Queens (as my local dry cleaner, Habana-San Juan, is currently doing after twenty-five years in three different locations on the Upper

West Side—each location smaller than the space before, and the last further from the main thoroughfare than the previous two. There are fewer Hispanics here than before, the owner is older, he lives in Queens, and has been commuting to this neighborhood at seven in the morning for more than two decades and is tired of it). But infrastructural forces will determine whether the landlord has three bids from white-owned businesses for the same space two months before his long-term Puerto Rican dry cleaner tenant leaves—or whether the same space will sit vacant for the next eighteen months with a crack across the glass behind the window gate.

§F. One of the problems with getting people to accept the first tenet of Marxism (infrastructure determines superstructure) is that we can look around us and *see* superstructural forces feeding back into the infrastructure and making changes in it. Because we are the "political size" we are (and thus have the political horizons we do), it's hard for individuals to see the extent of (or lack of) those changes. We have no way to determine by direct observation whether those changes are stabilizing/destabilizing or causative. And when we are unsure of (or wholly ignorant of) the infrastructural forces involved, often we assume that the superstructural forces that we have seen at work are responsible for major (i.e., infrastructural) changes. Infrastructural forces, however, often must be ferreted out and knowledge of their existence and effects disseminated by the superstructure.

That is to say, infrastructural forces will determine whether most of the neighborhood perceives Habana-San Juan's closing as another Puerto Rican business going as the neighborhood improves—or as another business-in-general folding as the neighborhood declines.

Infrastructure makes society go. Superstructure makes society go smoothly (or bumpily).

To confuse a stabilizing mechanism for a producing mechanism is to create all the problems a mechanic might have confusing a gyroscope for an internal combustion engine, or a farmer confusing his sack of fertilizer for his bag of seeds. (In the field of human endeavor language is a stabilizing mechanism, not a producing mechanism—regardless of what both artists and critics would prefer. This in no way contradicts the notion that the world to which we have access is constituted entirely of language, i.e., that it is constituted entirely by the structure of its stabilizing forces. All else is metaphysics.)

Again and again, however, such confusion causes people who should know better to decide that, because they have located some pervasive superstructural pattern (a prevalence of petty street crime in neighborhood X, say), superstructure here is actually *producing* all the visible infrastructural changes ("There was an influx of Puerto Ricans in neighborhood X, and a subsequent rise in drugs and petty street crimes; because of this, eventually the neighborhood was driven down till it became an all but abandoned slum where nobody, not even the Puerto Ricans, would live anymore . . ."), when, at the infrastructural level, what has actually happened is that landlords-as-a-class have realized that the older buildings in neighborhood X require more maintenance and thus a greater expenditure, so that they concentrate all their economic interest on newer properties with larger living units in neighborhood Y to the east, which is popular with young white upwardly mobile executives. The result is the decline of neighborhood X, of which street crime, drugs, and so on are only a symptom—though, as superstructural elements, those symptoms stabilize (i.e., help to assure) that decline and combat any small local attempts to reverse it by less than a major infrastructural change.

Finally, there is an important rider to the corollary: In much the same way as are contact and networking, infrastructure and superstructure are finally relative terms. They are vector processes rather than fixed positions, so that there *are* some locations where, depending on the vectors around them, for brief periods sometimes it is indeterminate whether something will operate with superstructural or infrastructural force. These are important intervention points, but they are not particularly germane to the analysis at hand, though an awareness of that importance makes me a marxian, rather than a Marxist.

Many commentators write about superstructural elements most people speak and write of *not* as stabilizing (or destabilizing) but as formative on the infrastructural level—whereas I have chosen to ignore them because they are *only* stabilizing or destabilizing. Thus at a number of places this argument may look incomplete. One example of the sort of thing I set aside is how much of the "lure" of Times Square was precisely *because* so much of its activity was illicit. But alluring illicit-ness is a superstructural result of infrastructure—stabilizing, certainly, but still not causative.

In an army jet, it is sometimes hard for a civilian passenger to tell whether she is hearing the engine or the gyroscope. The gyroscope is in the body of the plane. Both of them, running, make a fair amount of noise. Moreover, if you turn off the gyroscope, the plane will start to bounce around and buck through the air. In rough weather, this can be very disconcerting—leaving the civilian to think something awful has happened to the "motor."

Nevertheless, what makes the plane fly is *still* the jet engine.

§7.33. There is a conservative, stabilizing discourse already in place that sees in-terclass contact as the source of pretty much everything dangerous, unsafe, or un-desirable in the life of the country right now—from AIDS and "perversion" in all its forms, to the failures of education and neighborhood decay, to homelessness and urban violence. This discourse stabilizes the rhetoric in its particular anti-AIDS, antisex and anticrime (and even pro-theater) form that the infrastructural changes are generating, even though anyone familiar with the Times Square area can see that what is going on has nothing to do with this rhetoric and often contradicts it so flagrantly as to produce some Kafkaesque, if not Orwellian, nightmares.

Because of this discourse, any social form (or, indeed, architectural form) that shies us away from contact and contact-like situations and favors networking or relatively more network-like situations is likely to be approved. (The shift in pop-ularity from professional sports to university sports is a shift from a comparatively contact-oriented audience to a comparatively network-oriented audience; the growing audience for professional wrestling, however, represents an audience more amenable to contact. The split is—but certainly not entirely—a middle-class/working-class split, as well.) And more and more of the middle classes flock to networking situations, looking for the break, the chance, the pleasure, the lucky encounter, the hand up that will allow them to move through social, class, and/or economic strata—breaks, chances, pleasures, and lucky encounters that networking is not set up to provide, and often specifically retards.

§7.41. I hope—and hope very much—that the New Times Square works. Because cities function the way they do, however, *if* it works, parts of it will work by accident. Mr. Stern says that his employers want to promote more economic diversity. Well, I have to ask: More diversity relative to what? Certainly not to the old Times Square. Take the now completed section of the north face of the block between Seventh and Eighth Avenues: In the old Times Square, there was a cigar store on the corner, followed by a tie store, followed by a working entrance to a theater whose main body was around on Seventh Avenue, followed by another small clothing store, then the Brandt Theater, followed by the Victory Theater: that is to say, there were six commercial spaces, three of which were theaters and three of which were small sales outlets.

Along that same stretch of the New Times Square, there is Ferarra's on the corner (selling pastry and coffee). Last October, the next commercial space was occupied by a shop called Shade (which sold sun hats and sunglasses), but already it's out of business. Its papered-over store window currently announces,

§G. The neighborhoods that have best exploited the principles of variety, self-policing, and contact are (at least in Jacobs's view in 1961) those which have come about without particular planning. But if I have left any readers with the impression that, therefore, the

Coming Soon! The Brooklyn Pastrami Company. But the fact that one business has already folded in the New Times Square on what is supposed to be one of the world's busiest corners is *not* a good sign. This site is followed by Dapy (which sells a variety of tourist junk), followed by Magic Max, a magic store (there

165

"opposition" between contact and networking is somehow allied to an "opposition" between the planned and the architecturally unplanned (and that I am somehow on the side of "the unplanned"), then they will have doubly misread me.

The problem is (and the argument is presented by Jacobs as well) that our tradition of city planning goes back through some of the great architectural heros of modernity (like Le Corbusier) to the Victorian "garden city." That tradition operates by and continues to enforce two general assumptions, all but unquestioned.

The first assumption is: Since cities are fundamentally ugly places, the best way to combat this ugliness is to make them look as little like cities as possible. That means we hide the small, the poor, the dirty, the grubby—shrugging them off to the edges, putting them behind a veil of park land or public greenery. The assumption goes on: The best city neighborhoods are those that look as little like cities as possible. The *best* the city can produce is the boring, boring suburb.

The second assumption is: The only thing of intrinsic interest in the city is the gigantic, the colossal, the monumental. This alone

has traditionally been a magic store in the area; for years it was at the Eighth Avenue end of the block, down in the subway entrance); after that is the New Victory Theater, on the site of the old Victory: that's five commercial spaces—one theater and four stores. The drop from six to five is a drop of almost 17 percent. Certainly prices, goods, and other factors will contribute to economic diversity. But the architectural separation of the space represents a fairly firm "bottom line" beyond which diversity cannot go, unless those spaces are further broken up.

Nostalgia for the earlier six spaces over the current five is no more in question here than some fancied nostalgia for a half dozen years of rampant underage crack prostitution in the mid-eighties. Rather, what we are speaking of is the public presentation of the square by its developers, who say the builders are trying to promote economic diversity (when they are designing for relative economic homogeneity), or that they are opposed to drugs or violence against women, in order to make us feel that the project has some benefits for us. I am only pointing out that they have already—ruthlessly and vigorously—promoted all three (drugs, violence, and underage prostitution) in the pursuit of is what makes a city interesting, great, unique.

The approach to planning I propose flies in the face of both these assumptions as principles—with the result that, at least to most people at first, it may *look* like no planning at all.

Today our zoning practices are overwhelmingly exclusionary. They function entirely to keep different kinds of people, different kinds of business, different kinds of income levels and social practices from intermingling.

I suggest that we start putting together policies that mandate, rather, a sane and wholesome level of diversity in as many urban venues as possible.

New York Mayor Giuliani's current plan to move all sex business to the Westside waterfront area with a zoning mandate that each of the businesses must be at least five hundred feet from any other is a perfect example of the exclusionary policies I am protesting. The "five hundred foot" rule not only makes such businesses relatively difficult to access for the people who use them; it also makes them harder to police in any effective way. The dispersal coupled with the general desertedness at night of the neighbor-

what they are after. The idea that they will suddenly turn around and actually oppose them for any reason other than profit is, once more, naive.

§7.42. An example of (nonsexual) contact in Times Square:

While I was walking around the area this past summer, a young man taking pictures engaged me in conversation. A graduate student at the Columbia School of Journalism, he was there taking pictures and researching a thesis on the current reconstruction of the Times Square area. We chatted for about ten minutes. Then I left. The next day, passing through the square again, again I saw the young man with his camera. Again we said hello. Again we chatted some. This time we exchanged addresses. When I got home I mailed him an earlier version of this essay, as I had told him I would, as well as an extra copy I had of *Policing Public Sex*, which I'd mentioned to him as a useful volume but which he had not yet read.

Since the publishers had sent me two copies, as well as a set of galleys, I was perfectly happy to send one on to him.

I do not know if his thesis benefited from either our talk, this essay, or the book. We have hood to which these businesses are being confined makes those in the area far more vulnerable to street crimes. This seems to be planned punishment for those who will use the services of these businesses on foot in the after-work hours when most people will get to them. As well, it privileges car visits (because being in a car will be safer) in a city that is desperately trying to discourage excess vehicular traffic.

It would be far more sensible to encourage the sex businesses to clump. At the same time, eating places, other entertainment venues, drugstores, groceries, and living spaces should be encouraged to mix in among them. With such a policy set in place as part of a long-term plan, it might well encourage a new, lively bohemian living and entertainment neighborhood for the city.

Certainly, I would say, build for large commercial spaces along the street level. But intersperse them with smaller commercial spaces that will hold the human services that make utilizing the larger services pleasant.

My approach is not to forbid the towering office building, but rather to make sure that there is a variety of housing not only nearby

not run into one another since. But I can certainly hope.

A conservative commentator might ask, "Well, why are these beneficial nonsexual (i.e., safe) encounters threatened by the severe restriction of sexual (i.e., unsafe) encounters, especially if, as you say, the sexual ones are in the minority?"

My answer:

Desire is just as inseparable from the public contact situation as we have already seen in the fundamental structure of the networking situation. Desire and knowledge (body and mind) are *not* a fundamental opposition; rather, they are intricately imbricated and mutually constitutive aspects of political and social life. Situations of desire (as Freud noted in *Leonardo da Vinci and a Memory of His Childhood* [1910]) are the first objects and impellers of intellectual inquiry. Our society has responded to this in many ways, from putting the novel and poetry at the center of our study of the humanities to developing the old Times Square area at the center of the city that has been called the Capital of the Twentieth Century in much the way Paris is called the Capital of the Nineteenth Century.

But we might give more thought to the necessary and productive aspect of this im-but *intermixed with* such undertakings. And that means housing on several social levels.

Cities are attractive to businesses because of transportation, availability of materials, and skilled workers. Cities are attractive to *people* because of the pleasures the city holds. Much of that pleasure is cultural, certainly. Jobs are necessary to afford those pleasures. But when the average male thinks about sex once every thirty seconds and the average female thinks about sex once every three minutes, pretty much throughout their lives, it is absurd to think that sexual pleasure and sexual opportunity are somehow exempt from the equations that make city life attractive and livable.

brication of knowledge and desire as it expresses itself so positively in so many forms of contact, before—with a wrecking ball and even more sweeping legislation—we render that central structure asexual and "safe" in the name of family values and corporate giantism.

§7.43. The nature of the social practices I am interrogating is such that specific benefits and losses cannot be systematized, operationalized, standardized, or predicted. I can no more promise you a vacuum cleaner than I can an in-training marathon runner to return your pocketbook or a relevant volume for your research in the mail out of the blue. Even less can I say that no one will *ever* do anything nice for you at a professional gathering! What I *am* saying, however, is that most people—especially those who live in cities—if they look over the important occurrences in their lives over a substantial period of time, will likely notice that a substantial number of the important or dramatic ones, material or psychological, first arrived through strangers encountered in public spaces. This tendency is not an accident. It is a factor of the relative concentration of specific needs and suppliers in various social venues.

Networking situations start by gathering a population all with the same or relatively similar needs. While this concentration creates a social field that promotes the rapid spread of information among the members *about* those needs, the relatively high concentration of need itself militates against those needs being materially met within the networking situation—indeed, militates against their being met until the members physically abandon the network group and disperse into other venues.

Without in any way disparaging the excellences, pleasures, and rewards of small-town life, one must still acknowledge: The greater population and subsequently greater variety of needs and beneficial excesses to be found in cities make public contact venues, from the social to the sexual, a particularly important factor for social movement, change, and a generally pleasant life in a positive and pleasant democratic urban atmosphere.

§7.44. When I say I hope Times Square will work, my major fear is that the developers themselves do not know that they are lying. It is only the very young (who have seen too many mob movies) who believe criminals make better businessmen than fools. The fact is, there is just as large a percentage of foolish criminals as there is of foolish businessmen. Those who have *seen* criminals in business usually don't like it any more than they like to see fools running things.

§H. Architect Robert Stern has pointed out that the aura of theatricality about the Times Square area because of the theater district is a marvelous and vivid attraction not only to the neighborhood but to the whole city.

I don't know if this analysis has been done by the developers, but that aura is made to glow by three forces: (1) the glamour and excitement of the image of entertainment; (2) the underlying image of the theater as art, as site of social critique and topicality, of dissemination of important social images;

Theoreticians like Jacobs have given us some conceptual tools to understand the workings of certain city functions that, before her books, were largely invisible. It would be warming to think that developers might use those principles to produce profitable and vigorous urban spaces. What I'm afraid may happen is, however, that they are willing to gamble on the very high possibility that, after the immediate profits of the sweetheart deals that have allowed them to build their Brave New Mall, they will take the money and run, having bamboozled the rest of us into letting them build another artificial, overextended and (3) the money that we all know accrues to successful stars, successful producers, and successful works. The theater requires all three of these to maintain its aura. Remove any one, and theater becomes that much less attractive, appealing to a more limited group.

During the Buell Center conference where Stern spoke of his employers' "Ten Year Plan to Promote Theater and the Arts," theater critic Frank Rich, in his own presentation, pointed out that the organization of the legitimate theaters is moribund, with the two corporations that divide New York's legitimate Broadway theaters between them, the Schubert Organization and the Neiderlander Company, both on their last legs. Because of current Broadway costs, only a handful of Broadway theaters can even afford to run a full-scale musical. Even if most of the theaters are sold out nightly weeks on end, the houses are too small to support the running costs of an elaborate production today. Thus most of the theaters on Broadway are already considered by the companies that lease them "throwaway" theaters.

Should you want to experience that moribundity of the theater firsthand, sit on the steps of the downtown graveyard. The reason the famous four office towers were temporarily condensed to one (a fact that seems to warm Marshal Berman's heart)—with an "interim ten-year plan to promote theater and entertainment" that is pure Orwellian Newspeak—was that they would be impossible to rent. In the seventies the fact was given enough media play to discourage investors. The Times Square renovations have already demolished some thirty theater and film spaces in some thirty separate buildings in the area—and refurbished two: plans are to replace the destroyed spaces with *two* multiplex theater buildings. And at the end of the ten years? The four towers *will* be built.

§8.0. In 1992 we emerged from twelve years of a national Republican administration that favored big business—with the result that we now have some very strong big businesses indeed. The argument the Reagan/Bush leaders used to convince the public that this was a Good Thing was the promise of tax cuts and the "trickle-down" economic theory. The "trickle-down" economic theory, you may recall, was the notion that somehow big business would be helpful and supportive to small businesses.

permanently closed Biltmore Theater on Forty-seventh Street, beside the metal gate the bottom of
which has been eaten away with
uric acid, and chat with one of the
homeless men who regularly sleep
on a piece of cardboard under the
dark marquee during the summer.
Go along Thirty-ninth Street along
the theater back, where a dozen
homeless men and women huddle
or sleep in a welter of cardboard
and garbage.

The best thing that could happen to the theater district is that,
on the eventual breakup of the organizations, the theaters are sold
off to a number of smaller and
competing organizations. A number of the city's many theatrical ex-
perimental groups—La Mama, the
Manhattan Theater Club, the Theater for the New City, Westbeth,
CBA in Brooklyn, the LAB—should
be *given* Broadway outlets, among
precisely those theaters that Rich
noted as too small to produce
megaprofits. I do not think there is
anything nostalgic or any yearning
for authenticity in my suggestion
that what is far more likely to happen, however, is that the remnants
of the organizations will be bought
up by a single megacorporation,
and the "throwaway" theaters will
go the way of the old Helen Hayes

It has taken a half dozen years for New
Yorkers to learn, at least, what anyone over
thirty-five could have told them in 1980 when
Reagan was elected: Big businesses drive out
small businesses. Left unsupervised, big businesses stamp out small businesses, break them
into pieces, devour the remains, and dance
frenziedly on their graves. Now that we have
watched Barnes and Noble destroy Books and
Company on the East Side and Shakespeare
and Company on the West and, in my own
neighborhood, seen the Duane Reade Phar-
macy chain put Lasky's and Ben's and several
other small drugstores out of business, people
have some models for the quality of service
and the general atmosphere of pleasant interchange to be lost when big businesses destroy
small ones.

Small businesses thrive on contact—the
word-of-mouth reputations that contact engen-
ders: "You're looking for X? Try Q's. It's really
good for what you want."

Big businesses promote networking as
much as they possibly can: "Shop at R's—and
be part of today!" vibrating over the airwaves in
a three-million-dollar ad campaign.

In one sense, the Times Square takeover is
one of the larger and more visible manifesta-
tions of the small being obliterated by the large.

and the Morosco, torn down to make way for more office buildings and hotels. (For all this love for the theater, under pressure from the Forty-second Street Development Project or its avatars, since 1980, at least five theater buildings in the area have already been pulled down [the old Helen Hayes, the Morosco, the Adonis, the Circus, and one on the south side of Forty-second between Sixth and Seventh, whose name I cannot find out] and five more [including the Capri, the Eros I, the Cameo, the Venus, and two on the north side of Forty-second Street between Sixth and Seventh] have been totally remodeled into something that can never be used as theatrical space again. Nor does this count any of the nine theaters on Forty-second Street that stand closed and awaiting demolition. Since that time, one theater has been built—the New Victory children's theater—and one, the New Amsterdam, has been renovated. This should give the lie to any protestations of serious concern with theater in New York made by any spokesperson of the Forty-second Street Development Project. What the project wants to do is exactly what its managers wanted to do in the 1970s when this plan got

We are in a period of economic growth, we all know. But most of us are asking, Why, then, isn't *my* life more pleasant? The answer is that "pleasantness" is controlled by small business diversity and social contact; and in a democratic society that values social movement, social opportunity, and class flexibility, interclass contact is the most rewarding, productive, and thus privileged kind of contact. There is no way people can move comfortably between classes if the classes themselves do not have repeated, pleasant social interactions with one another, class war or not.

Big business is anti-contact in the same way that it is anti–small business. But there are many tasks that small businesses—like bookstores, stationery stores, and, often, drugstores—can do more efficiently for the customers and more pleasantly (that word again) than can big businesses and large chain outlets.

And, again, certain benefits from contact, networking simply *cannot* provide.

§8.1. An academic who heard an earlier version of this argument told me that it explained a family phenomenon that, in his younger years, had puzzled and sometimes embarrassed him.

"Whenever we would go with my grandfather to a restaurant—my grampa had been

173

under way: build its office towers and its mall—and preserve a handful of theaters as museum pieces . . . only because they don't think they can get away with destroying them all.) The remaining theaters will be, at best, theatrical museums for more glitzy productions of *Guys and Dolls, Grease,* and *The King and I,* and, at their worst, new and bigger and more gorgeous productions referring to less and less of the social and material world around us. The amount and variety of Broadway theater will be drastically reduced—and with it will go the aura of theatricality that Mr. Stern has cited as one of our city's most valuable assets.

born and grew up in Italy—within ten minutes, he had everybody in the restaurant talking not only to him but to everybody else."

The question in his grandson's mind: "Why do you always have to *do* that, Gramps?"

The answer, he realized from my talk: How else did an unlettered laborer such as his grandfather in the 1930s and 1940s go into a new neighborhood, a new area, and get work?

A reasonable argument might be made that a notable percentage of the homeless population in our cities today is comprised of men and women who grew up in social enclaves that counted on contact relations to provide those prized necessities, jobs, shelter, and friendship—a social practice at which,

often, we can still see that they were very good—but who were unsuited, both by temperament and education, for the more formal stringencies of networking relations. In networking situations, one secures work and social necessities through want ads, résumés, recommendations, job applications, real estate listings, and social interest groups, a mode of social practice that, in urban venue

§I. Because isolated low-level optionless poverty that shifts between poor homes and the very bottom of the job system (where the "system" itself is seen as a fundamentally bureaucratic network phenomenon) has been called "feminized," one is tempted to call "masculinized!" that homeless poverty

after urban venue, has displaced contact relations ("You want a job? Show up tomorrow morning at six-thirty: I'll put you to work.") till there are hardly any left. Indeed, it is my deep suspicion that the only consistent and ultimately necessary learning that occurs across the field of "universal higher education" toward which our country leans more where people drop through the system's very bottom into a world where ever-shrinking contact opportunities are the only social relations available. One of Gordon's points was that more and more men find themselves caught up in "feminized" poverty structures. Well, many, many women and children are on the streets barely surviving, suffering, and dying in "masculinized" poverty. Myself, I think that the gendering of such states merely overwrites and erases contextual power divisions and questions of wealth deployment with vague suggestions of a wholly inappropriate, bogus, and mystifying psychologization (men *choose* one kind of poverty; women *choose* another; when poverty is precisely about *lack* of choices)— and so should be discouraged, however well-intentioned it all first seems.

and more is the two to four years of acclimation to the bureaucratic management of our lives that awaits more and more of the country's working classes—and that goes along directly with (if it is not the institutional backbone of) Richard Gordon's analysis of the "homework economy" and the "feminization of poverty," which Donna Haraway brought to our attention more than a decade ago in her widely read essay "A Cyborg Manifesto."

§8.2. What has happened to Times Square has already made my life, personally, somewhat more lonely and isolated. I have talked with a dozen men whose sexual outlets, like many of mine, were centered on that neighborhood. It is the same for them.

We need contact.

In these notes I have tried to go over some of the material and economic forces that work—on Forty-second Street and in general— to suppress contact in the name of "giving people what they want." I hope I've made it clear: The erosion of contact on Forty-second Street is only an instance of a larger trend, in which sex is involved in some places and in others not—though desire and/or the fear of desire works through them all.

How can we promote more contact—and possibly even reverse this trend?

Education is certainly one factor—particularly education about the way complex social units, such as cities and city neighborhoods, function. People about to come to the city need a more realistic view of what they will find when they get here. Most important, they must be disabused of the notion of the city as a unified and pervasive place of homogenized evil—as well as the equally false image that the Forty-second Street Development Project would replace it with: the image of a space of pervasive and homogenized safety.

Those images are, of course, simpler to hold on to than the politically more useful ones, which tell us that in general the city is a pretty safe place, though the violence that occurs there is largely random. There are certainly specific types of big-city smarts (walking next to the curb on dark streets; listening, on sparsely populated streets, to make sure the group of people coming up behind you are engaged in conversation; a sense of what streets to avoid at which hours). Those areas where violence may be reasonably expected with some frequency (often the first place the tourist sees: The bus station, the train station, the streets around Times Square) tend to operate on a largely small-town model and thus can usually be negotiated with ordinary (dare I say it) small-town common sense. But the comparative urban paucity of violence is among the most powerful factors constituting the freedom of action and thought—so often called opportunity—that small towns simply cannot proffer.

§8.3. City dwellers need to be educated as well. Investors need to know more about the economics of large-scale real estate construction. They need to know that investors alone depend on the final success of the building for their returns, while the corporation overseeing the actual construction need only be concerned with getting the object built in order to make substantial profits. City dwellers need to be educated to the necessity of contact and contact venues. As well, they need to have a clear notion of why contact *cannot* be replaced with networking institutions in some ill-conceived attempt to sidestep urban violence.

In the name of family values, safety, and profits, developers are designing the new mall of New York to suppress as much street contact as they possibly can, however vital it is to city life. In no way is this *just* Times Square's problem. It is the multi-urban problem of the country, and it arises anywhere that American designers have stepped in to model various civic centers. The reason we allow and even encourage it is that people do not understand the workings of urban mechanisms. Believing that networking institutions can supply the same or even better benefits than contact, we have been convinced that we *should* fear contact.

People educated in the realities of city functioning must make *their* demands—and their fears—articulate. Because we have a system where the public's perception is, indeed, as powerful as it is (it can put off a greedy, money-grabbing set of construction deals by a decade), it can also promote the planning and construction of civic spaces designed to encourage contact rather than discourage it, and make it appear a profit-making process. (A park surrounded only by residences, especially towering apartments, soon becomes a locked fortress like Gramercy Park and/or a criminal inferno like the central parks in so many low-cost housing projects. A park sided by a variety of human services, including coffee shops and inexpensive restaurants liberally intermixed with residences and other commercial establishments soon becomes a self-policing venue that promotes relaxed anxiety-free use—and urban contact.) We have to educate people to look not so much at social objects and social monuments but to observe, analyze, and value a whole range of social relationships.

§8.4. Because of its topological site in the city, the Times Square area—the major entrance and exit to and from the city, thanks to the Port Authority and the Lincoln Tunnel—is the perfect place to encourage all forms of entertainment *and* desire.

§8.5. City planners, architects, and the people who commission them must be alerted to the long-term benefits—the social necessity—of designing for diversity:

Large and small must be built side by side.

Living spaces, commercial spaces, eating establishments, repair spaces, and entertainment spaces must all be intermixed.

Large businesses and offices must alternate with small businesses and human services, even while places to live at all levels, working-class, middle-class, and luxurious, large and small, must embraid with them into a community.

This flies in the face of more than a hundred years of architectural practice. Our society wants to condense, distill, centralize, and giantize. But when this becomes a form—*the* form—of social engineering, whether in the form of upper-class residential neighborhoods with no stores and no working-class residences, whether in the form of business neighborhoods with no residences at all, or in the form of industrial neighborhoods with no white-collar businesses and no stores, the result is a social space that can do well only as long as money is poured constantly into it. Such locations have no way of producing the economic cushioning that holds things stable at the infrastructural level. While such neighborhoods may be, at their outset, provisionally convenient, or uncrowded, or even beautiful, they can never remain pleasant to move around in over any extended period. Without a web of social pleasantry, uncrowded soon becomes lonely; beautiful becomes artificial; and even the convenience of propinquity transforms into the oppressing necessity to be where one would rather not. Under such valuative shifts, all too quickly follow those material transformations wrought by time alone, where neat and well cared for become abandoned, dirty, filled with trash, and rundown, while another neighborhood, three times or five times or ten times as old, which has nevertheless been able to maintain that stabilizing web of lived social pleasantry and diversity, is perceived—however shabby it may be—as quaint and full of historical interest.

What I and many other small voices are proposing is that we utilize consciously the same principles of socioeconomic diversity through which those pleasant, various, and stable neighborhoods that were never planned grew up naturally. Purposely we must reproduce those multiform and variegated social levels to achieve like neighborhoods as ends.

If our ideal is to promote movement among the classes and the opportunity for such movement, we can do it only if we create greater propinquity among the different elements that make up the different classes.

That *is* diversity.

Today, however, diversity has to claw its way into our neighborhoods as an afterthought—often as much as a decade after the places have been built and thought out. (It is not just that there were once trees and public ashtrays on Forty-second Street between Seventh and Eighth Avenues. There were also an apartment house and grocery stores, an automat, a sporting goods store, clothing stores, bookstores, electronics stores, a cigar store and several newsstands, and half a dozen restaurants at various levels, all within a handful of meters of the Candler office tower—as well as the dozen movie theaters and amusement halls [Fascination, Herbert's Flea Circus], massage parlors and sex shows for which the area was famous, for almost fifty years—fifty years that encompassed the heyday and height of the strip as the film and entertainment capital of the city, of the world.) Why not begin by designing *for* such variety?

At the human level, such planned diversity promotes—as it stabilizes the quality of life and the long-term viability of the social space—human contact.

§9. Here's a composite entry from my journal for spring '97.

§10. After a trip to the Thirty-fourth Street Central Post Office to mail a book to a friend, I walked up Eighth Avenue to the Port Authority, where I stopped to speak to Todd—of the spectacularly missing front tooth. His clothes were clean and his shirt was new, but he is still homeless, he explained. (In his mid-thirties, he has been for over a decade.) Just come from a stint sleeping on the subway, he asked me for some change to get something to eat. I gave him a handful that probably totaled about a dollar seventy-five. "Oh, thanks, man," he said. "Now I can go get me some chicken wings."

I was in the city to participate in a three-day conference on "Forms of Desire" at the Center for Lesbian and Gay Studies (CLAGS) at the SUNY Graduate Center. It's April, and after the snowstorm on the first, warmer weather seemed to have doubled the daytime Times Square traffic. Ben was back from vacation with his wife and setting up his shoeshine stand behind the subway kiosk on the northeast corner. To the southwest, under the Port's marquee, Anthony Campbell was taking the afternoon shift. And Christos was there, among the pretzel and hot dog vendors, with his shish kebab wagon. (More and more these days he leaves the actual running of the stand to a Pakistani assistant.) Darrell and Dave have not been in evidence awhile now. Back in January and February, I'd run into Darrell a few times, either on the corner or coming out of the peep shows further up Eighth Avenue. Street life wasn't so good for him, he admitted. But the long-awaited publication of the picture in *OUT Magazine,* he told me, had opened up some model work for him with the *Latin Connection*. Months ago, someone introduced him to some filmmakers (pure networking), but the *OUT* photo (pure contact) apparently pushed them to act on his application a lot more quickly.

I hope things go well for him.

Back in January I saw Dave over on Ninth Avenue, running after drugs. ("Hey there, man! Hey, there! So long!") But not since.

There on the crowded corner, however, Lenny and Jeff and Frank were still hanging out—even while a scuffle between two young men created a widening circle under the Port's marquee, till a sudden surge of police tightened it into a knot of attention. A policeman sped past my shoulder through the crowd, while the woman beside him shrieked. Then, for a solid minute, the knot pulled tight enough to become impenetrable to sight. Moments later, however, the same policeman led away a white kid in a blue-checked shirt, with a backwards baseball cap and a bleeding face (as he stumbled in the policeman's grip, he bumped against

Christos's stand) while a Hispanic kid in a red jacket, shaking his head, talked to some other policeman. Beside me, tall Frank told me, "Wow! They *got* him. They actually caught him. Man, that was cool. I didn't think they were going to get him. But they caught him!" Like Jeff, Frank, a longtime hustler on that corner, has no brief for violence that might keep his customers away.

The third evening after the conference, at the back of the 104 Broadway bus, half a dozen riders (four middle-aged women, two middle-aged men), each with his or her copy of *Playbill*, spontaneously began to discuss the matinees they'd seen that afternoon. In the full bus, the conversations wound on, and I found myself talking to a woman next to me down from Connecticut, also just from the theater. It is spring and New York is full of contact, though I note that the conversation in the back of the bus was not cross-class contact, but pretty well limited to folks who could afford the sixty or seventy dollars for a Broadway ticket, and so partook a bit more of the economic context of networking—the *Playbills* acting as signs of the shared interest (and shared economic level) characteristic of a networking group. Also, characteristic of networking groups, what circulated among them was knowledge of what actors seemed good, what plays seemed strong or enjoyable, which musicals had good voices but weak songs, and which just did not seem worth the time to attend.

Let me be specific. In the ten years I've known Todd, I'm sure the handouts I've given him, a dollar here, two dollars there (say, once a month), easily total $180 or more—that is, over twice the price of a Broadway show ticket. If, on the bus, however, one of the *Playbill* wavers were to ask me or one of the others with whom she had been chatting amiably, "Say, here's my name and address. The next time you're going to the theater, just pick up an extra ticket and drop it in the mail to me," it would bring the conversation to a stunned halt; and however the theater-going passengers might have dealt with it in the public space of a twenty-minute bus ride, certainly no one would have seriously acceded to the request.

That is to say, once again, the material rewards from street contact (the quintessential method of the panhandler) are simply greater, even if spread out over a decade, than the rewards from a session of networking—which rewards take place (I say again) largely in the realm of shared knowledge.

That evening, around seven-twenty, I got home to comet Hale-Bopp, bright and fuzzy-bearded above the west extremity of Eighty-second Street, against an indigo evening only a single shade away from full black. At the corner, I phoned up to Dennis in the apartment (one payphone was broken; I had to cross over to use the one on the far corner), who hadn't seen it yet, to come out and take a look. Two minutes later he was down on the stoop. To prepare him, I pointed out a couple of diamond-chip stars overhead. "Now that's a star. And *that's* a star. But if you look over there—"

Without my even pointing, he declared, "Wow, *there* it is!"—the fuzzy starlike object with its gauzy beard of light fanning to the east (I'd first seen it on my birthday, two nights before, up in Massachusetts).

Dennis dashed back up to get his binoculars and go check it out from our roof; I turned up the street to make a quick trip to the supermarket. On my way back down Eighty-second Street, Hale-Bopp created a veritable wave of contact.

First an overheard father and two kids, son and daughter: "Hey, do you see the comet up there . . . ?"

"Yeah, I saw it last week."

Moments on, I pointed it out to a heavy, white-haired plainclothes policeman lounging in jeans and blue sweatshirt by the gate up at the precinct, who responded, "Do I see it? Sure. It's right up there, isn't it?"

Which turned two women around in their tracks, one in a brown raincoat, both in hats. "Is *that* it? Oh, yes."

"Yes, right there. *My!*"

"You can really see it tonight! Maybe we should go down to the river and look."

I left the policeman explaining to them why they *didn't* want to do that.

Thirty yards further down the block, I pointed it out to a stocky young Hispanic couple who passed me hand in hand: "Yeah, sure. We already seen it."

A minute later I pointed it out again to a homeless man in his twenties with blackened hands and short black hair, who'd set his plastic garbage bag down to dig in a garbage container for soda and beer cans. "Oh, wow! Yeah—" slowly he stood up to rub his forehead—"that's neat!" While I walked on, a moment later I glanced back to see he'd stopped an older Hispanic gentleman in an overcoat, with a pencil-thin mustache, who now stood with him, gazing up: "There, you see the comet . . . ?"

With my cane, I walked up my stoop steps, carrying my groceries and my notebook into the vestibule, where I unlocked the door and pushed into the lobby.

§10.1. How does this set of urban interactions beneath a passing celestial portent differ from similar encounters, possibly the same evening, a hundred or five hundred miles away, on some small-town street? First, these encounters are in a big city. Second, over the next eight months, I have seen none of the people involved in them again—neither the homeless man nor the Hispanic gentleman, the young couple nor the pair of women, nor the policeman (one among the seventy-five-odd officers who work out of the precinct at the far end of my block, perhaps fifteen of whom I know by sight). Their only fallout is that they were pleasant—and that pleasantness hangs in the street under the trees and by the brownstone stoops near which they occurred, months after Hale-Bopp has ellipsed the sun and soared again into solar night. That fallout will remain as long as I remain comfortable living here.

§10.2. Not a full year after the CLAGS "Forms of Desire" conference that took place under the auspices of Hale-Bopp and provoked the journal entry above, at the February 1998 OutWrite Conference of Lesbian and Gay Writers in Boston, one of the Sunday morning programs began with the two questions:

"Why is there homophobia?" and "What makes us gay?"

As I listened to the discussion over the next hour and a half, I found myself troubled: Rather than attack both questions head-on, both discussants tended to veer away from them, as if those questions were somehow logically congruent to the two great philosophical conundrums, ontological and epistemological, that ground Western philosophy—"Why is there something rather than nothing?" and "How can we know it?"—and, as such, could be approached only by elaborate indirection.

It seems to me (and this will bring the multiple arguments of this lengthy discussion to a close under the rubric of my third thesis: the mechanics of discourse) that there are pointed answers to be given to the questions "Why is there homophobia?" and "What makes us gay?"—answers that are imperative if gay and lesbian men and women are to make any progress in passing from what Urvashi Vaid has called, so tellingly, "virtual equality" (the appearance of equality with few or none of the material benefits) to a material and legal-based equality.

During the forties and fifties my uncle (my mother's brother-in-law) Myles Paige, a black man who had graduated from Tuskegee, was a Republican, a Catholic, and a respected judge in the Brooklyn Domestic Relations Court. By the time I was ten or eleven, I knew why "prostitutes and perverts" (my uncle was the first to join them for me in seductive alliteration; it is not without significance that, in the 1850s in London, "gays," the plural term for male homosexuals today, meant female prostitutes) were to be hated, if not feared. I was told the reason repeatedly during half a dozen family dinners, where, over the roast lamb, the macaroni and cheese, the creamed onions, and the kale, at the head of the family dinner table my uncle, the judge, held forth.

"Prostitutes and perverts," he explained, again and yet again, "destroy, undermine, and rot the foundations of society." I remember his saying (again and again) that if he had his way, "I would take all those people out and shoot 'em!" while his more liberal wife—my mother's sister—protested futilely. "Well," my uncle grumbled, "I *would* . . ." The implication was that he had some arcane and secret information about "prostitutes and perverts" that, while it justified the ferocity of his position, could not be shared at the dinner table with women and children. But I entered adolescence knowing that the law alone, and my uncle's judicial position in it, kept his anger, and by extension the anger of all right-thinking men like him, in check—kept it from breaking out in a concerted attack on "those people," who were destroying, undermining, and rotting the foundations of society, which meant, as far as I understood it, they were menacing my right to sit there in the dining room in the Brooklyn row house on Macdonnah Street and eat our generous, even lavish Sunday dinner that my aunt and grandmother had fixed over the afternoon.

These were the years between, say, 1949 and 1953, that I—and I'm sure, many, many others—heard this repeatedly as the general social judgment on sex workers and/or homosexuals. That is to say, it was about half a dozen years after the end of World War II. Besides being a judge, my Uncle Myles had also been a captain in the U.S. army.

What homosexuality and prostitution represented for my uncle was the untrammeled pursuit of pleasure; and the untrammeled pursuit of pleasure was the opposite of social responsibility. Nor was this simply some abstract principle for the generation so recently home from European military combat. Many had begun to wake, however uncomfortably, to a fact that problematizes much of the discourse around sadomasochism today. In the words of Bruce Benderson, writing in the *Lambda Book Report 12*, "The true Eden where all desires are satisfied is red, not green. It is a blood bath of instincts, a gaping maw of orality, and a basin of gushing bodily fluids." Too many had seen "nice ordinary American boys" let loose in some tiny French or German or Italian town where, with the failure of the social contract, there was no longer any law—and there had seen all too much of that red

185

"Eden." In World War II, these situations were not officially interrogated; no attempts were made to tame them for the public with images such as "Lt. Calley" and "My Lai," as they would be a decade and a half later in Vietnam. Rather, they circulated as an unstated and inarticulate horror whose lessons were supposed to be brought back to the States while their specificity was, in any collective narrativity, unspeakable, left in the foreign outside, safely beyond the pale.

The clear and obvious answer (*especially* to a Catholic Republican army officer and judge) was that pleasure must be socially doled out in minuscule amounts, tied by rigorous contracts to responsibility. Good people were people who accepted this contractual system. Anyone who rebelled *was* a prostitute or a pervert, or both. Anyone who actively pursued prostitution or perversion was working, whether knowingly or not, to unleash precisely those red Edenic forces of desire that could only topple society, destroy all responsibility, and produce a nation without families, without soldiers, without workers—indeed, a chaos that was itself no state, for clearly no such space of social turbulence could maintain any but the most feudal state apparatus.

That was and will remain the answer to the question, "Why is there hatred and fear of homosexuals (homophobia)?" as long as this is the systematic relation between pleasure and responsibility in which "prostitution and perversion" are seen to be caught up. The herd of teenage boys who stalk the street with their clubs, looking for a faggot to beat bloody and senseless, the employer who fires the worker who is revealed to be gay, the landlord who turns the gay tenant out of his or her apartment, or the social circle that refuses to associate with someone who is found out to be gay are simply the Valkyries—the *Wunchmaids*—to my uncle's legally constrained Woton.

What I saw in the conversation at OutWrite was that the argument exists today largely at the level of discourse, and that younger gay activists find it hard to articulate the greater discursive structure they are fighting to dismantle, as do those conservatives today who uphold one part of it or the other without being aware of its overall form. But discourses in such condition tend to remain at their most stable.

In order to dismantle such a discourse we must begin with the realization that desire is *never* "outside *all* social constraint." Desire may be outside one set of constraints or another; but social constraints are what engender desire; and, one way or another, even at its most apparently catastrophic, they contour desire's expression.

On the particular level where the argument must proceed case by case, incident by incident, before it reaches discursive (or counterdiscursive) mass, we must look at how that principle operates in the answer to our second question, "What makes us gay?"

The question "What makes us gay?" has at least three different levels on which answers can be posed.

First, the question "What makes us gay?" might be interpreted to mean "What do we do, what qualities do we possess, that signal the fact that we partake of the preexisting essence of 'gayness' that gives us our gay 'identity' and that, in most folks' minds, means that we belong to the category of 'those who are gay?'" This is, finally, the semiotic or epistemological level: How do we—or other people—know we are gay?

There is a second level, however, on which the question "What makes us gay?" might be interpreted: "What forces or conditions in the world take the potentially 'normal' and 'ordinary' person—a child, a fetus, the egg and sperm before they even conjoin as a zygote—and 'pervert' them (i.e., turn them away) from that 'normal' condition so that now we have someone who does some or many or all of the things we call gay—or at least wants to, or feels compelled to, even if she or he would rather not?" This is, finally, the ontological level: What makes these odd, statistically unusual, but ever-present gay people exist in the first place?

The confusion between questions one and two, the epistemological and the ontological, is already enough to muddle many arguments. People who think they are asking question two are often given (very frustrating) answers to question one, and vice versa.

But there is a third level where this question "What makes us gay?" can be interpreted that is often associated with queer theory and academics of a poststructuralist bent. Many such academics have claimed that their answer to (and thus their interpretation of) the question is the most important one, and that this answer absorbs and explains what is really going on at the first two levels.

This last is not, incidentally, a claim that I make. But I do think that this third level of interpretation (which, yes, is an aspect of the epistemological, but might be more intelligibly designated today as the theoretical) is imperative if we are to explain to a significant number of people what is wrong with a discourse that places pleasure and the body in fundamental opposition to some notion of a legally constrained social responsibility, rather than a discourse that sees that pleasure and the body are constitutive elements of the social as much as are law and responsibility.

One problem with this third level of interpretation of "What makes us gay?" that many of us academic folk have come up with is that it puts considerable strain in such a question on the ordinary meaning of "makes."

The argument against our interpretation might start along these lines (I begin here because, by the polemic against it, the reader may have an easier time recognizing it when it arrives in its positive form): "'To make' is an active verb. You seem to be describing a much more passive process. It sounds like you're describing some answer to the question 'What allows us to be gay?' or 'What facilitates our being gay?' or even 'What allows people to speak about people as gay?' Indeed, the answer you propose doesn't seem to have anything to do with 'making' at all. It seems to be all about language and social habit."

To which, if we're lucky enough for the opposition to take its objection to this point, we can answer back, "You're right! That's *exactly* our point. We now believe that language and social habit are much more important than heretofore, historically, they have been assumed to be. Both language and social habit perform many more jobs, intricately, efficiently, and powerfully, unto shaping not just what we call social reality, but even what we call reality itself (against which we used to set social reality in order to look at it as a separate situation from material reality). Language and social habit don't produce only the appearance of social categories: rich, poor, educated, uneducated, well-mannered, ill-bred—those signs that, according to Henry Higgins in *My Fair Lady*, can be learned and therefore faked. They produce as well what heretofore were considered ontological categories: male, female, black, white, Asian, straight, gay, normal, and abnormal . . . as well as trees, books, dogs, wars, money, rainstorms, and mosquitoes; and they empower us to put all those ironizing quotation marks around words like "normal," "ordinary," and "pervert" in our paragraph describing the ontological level.

Because we realize just how powerful the sociolinguistic process is, we *insist* on coupling it to those active verbs, "to make, to produce, to create," although, early in the dialogue, there was another common verb for this particular meaning of "make" that paid its due to the slow, sedentary, and passive (as well as inexorable and adamantine) quality of the process: "to sediment"—a verb that fell away because it did not suit the polemical nature of the argument, but which at this point it might be well to retrieve: "What makes us gay?" in the sense of "What produces us as gay? What creates us as gay? What sediments us as gay?"

The level where these last four questions overlap is the level where our interpretation of the question—and our answer to it—stands.

Consider a large ballroom full of people.

At various places around the walls there are doors. If one of the doors is open, and the ballroom is crowded enough, after a certain amount of time there will be a certain number of people in the other room on the far side of the open door (assuming the lights are on and nothing is going on in there to keep them out). The third-level theoretical answer to the question "What makes us gay?" troubles the ordinary man or woman on the street for much the same reason it would trouble

189

them if you said, of the ballroom and the room beside it, "The open door is what makes people go into the other room."

Most folks are likely to respond, "Sure, I *kind* of see what you mean. But aren't you just playing with words? Isn't it really the density of the ballroom's crowd, the heat, the noise, the bustle in the ballroom that drive (i.e., that *make*) people go into the adjoining room? I'm sure you could come up with experiments where, if, on successive nights, you raised or lowered the temperature and/or the noise level, you could even correlate them to how much faster or slower people were driven out of the ballroom and into the adjoining room—thus proving crowd, heat, and noise were the causative factors, rather than the door, which is finally just a facilitator, *n'est-ce pas?*"

The answer to this objection is "You're answering the question as though it were being asked at level two, the ontological level. And for level two, your answer is fine. The question *I* am asking, however, on level three, is 'What makes the people go into *that* room rather than any number of other possible rooms that they might have entered, behind any of the other *closed* doors around the ballroom?' And the actual answer to *that* question really *is* 'That particular *open* door.'"

It's time to turn to the actual and troubling answer that we have come up with to the newly interpreted question, "What makes us gay?" The answer is usually some version of the concept "We are made gay because that is how we have been interpellated."

"Interpellate" is a term that was revived by Louis Althusser in his 1969 essay, "Ideology and Ideological State Apparatuses." The word once meant "to interrupt with a petition." Prior to the modern era, the aristocrats who comprised many of the royal courts could be presented with petitions by members of the *haute bourgeoisie.* These aristocrats fulfilled their tasks as subjects to the king by reading over the petitions presented to them, judging them, and acting on them in accord with the petitions' perceived merit. Althusser's point is that "we become subjects when we are interpellated." In the same paragraph, he offers the word "hailed" as a syn-

onym, and goes on to give what has become a rather notorious example of a policeman calling out or hailing, "Hey, you!" on the street. Says Althusser, in the
process of saying, "He must mean me," we cohere into a self—rather than being,
presumably, simply a point of view drifting down the street.

That awareness of "he must mean me" is the constitutive *sine qua non* of
the subject. It is the mental door through which we pass into subjectivity and
selfhood. And (maintains Althusser) this cannot be a spontaneous process, but is
always a response to some hailing, some interpellation, by some aspect of the
social.

In that sense, it doesn't really matter whether someone catches you in the
bathroom, looking at a same-sex nude, and then blurts out, "Hey, you're gay!" and
you look up and realize "you" ("He means me!") have been caught, or if you're
reading a description of homosexuality in a textbook and "you" think, "Hey,
they're describing me!" The point is, rather, that anyone who self-identifies as gay
must have been interpellated, at some point, as gay by some individual or social
speech or text to which he or she responded, "He/she/it/they must mean me." That
is the door opening. Without it, nobody can say proudly, "I *am gay!*" Without it,
nobody can think guiltily and in horror, "Oh my God, I'm *gay!*" Without it, one
cannot remember idly or in passing, "Well, I'm gay."

Because interpellation talks about only one aspect of the meaning of "making"/"producing"/"creating"/"sedimenting," it does not tell the whole story. It is
simply one of the more important things that happen to subjects at the level of discourse. And, in general, discourse constitutes and is constituted by what Walter
Pater called, in the conclusion to *The Renaissance*, "a roughness of the eye." Thus,
without a great deal more elaboration, the notion of interpellation is as reductive
as any other theoretical move. But it locates a powerful and pivotal point in the
process. And it makes it clear that the process is, as are all the creative powers
of discourse, irrevocably anchored within the social, rather than somehow
involved with some fancied breaking out of the social into an uncharted and

unmapped beyond, that only awaits the release of police surveillance to erupt into that red Eden of total unconstraint.

Here is what the priority of the social says about those times in war where that vision of hell was first encountered by people like my uncle, possibly among our own soldiers: Look, if you spend six months socializing young men to "kill, kill, kill," it's naive to be surprised when some of them, in the course of their pursuit of pleasure, do. It is not because some essentialist factor in "perversion" or "prostitution" (or sexuality in general) always struggles to break loose.

It is language (and/as social habit) that cuts the world up into the elements, objects, and categories we so glibly call reality—a reality that includes the varieties of desire; a reality where what is real *is* what must be dealt with, which is one with the political: the world *is* what it is cut up into—all else is metaphysics. That is all that is meant by that troubling poststructuralist assertion that the world is constituted of and by language and nothing more that we have any direct access to.

The problem with this assertion is that one of the easiest things to understand about it is that if language/social habit makes/produces/sediments anything, it makes/produces/sediments the meanings of words. Thus, the meaning of "makes" on the semiological/epistemological level is a sociolinguistic sedimentation. The meaning of "makes" on the ontological level is a sociolinguistic sedimentation. And, finally, the meaning of "makes" on the theoretical (i.e., sociolinguistic) level is also a sociolinguistic sedimentation. This is all those who claim that the third meaning encompasses and explains the other two are saying. When I said above that I do not make that claim, what *I* was saying in effect was: I am not convinced that this is an important observation telling us something truly interesting about ontology or epistemology. It may just be an empty tautology that can be set aside and paid no more attention to. Personally, I think the decision as to whether it is or is not interesting is to be found *in* ontology and epistemology themselves— rather than in theory. That is to say, if the observation emboldens us to explore the world, cut it up in new and different ways, and learn what new and useful relationships can result, then the observation is of use and interest; but it is not interesting to the extent that it leads only to materially unattended theoretical restatements of itself.

§10.3. Following directly from my primary thesis, my primary conclusion is that, while still respecting the private/public demarcations (I do *not* believe that property is theft), we'd best try cutting the world up in different ways socially and rearranging it so that we may benefit from the resultant social relationships. For decades the governing cry of our cities has been "Never speak to strangers." I propose that in a democratic city it is imperative that we speak to strangers, live next to them, and learn how to relate to them on many levels, from the political to the sexual. City venues must be designed to allow these multiple interactions to occur easily, with a minimum of danger, comfortably, and conveniently. This is what politics—the way of living in the polis, in the city—is about.

While one thrust of this essay is that such catastrophic civic interventions as the Forty-second Street Development Project are based on the incorrect assumption that interclass contact is necessarily unsafe (it threatens to unleash the sexual, crime, mayhem, murder . . .) and that its benefits can be replaced by networking (safe, monitored, controlled, under surveillance . . .), a second thrust has been and is that social contact is of paramount importance in the specific pursuit of gay sexuality. The fact is, I am not interested in the "freedom" to "be" "gay" without any of the existing gay institutions or without other institutions that can take up and fulfill like functions.

Such "freedom" means nothing. Many gay institutions—clubs, bars of several persuasions, baths, tea-room sex, gay porn movie

§J. The Times Square renovation is not just about real estate and economics, however unpleasant its ramifications have been on that front. Because it has involved the major restructuring of the legal code relating to sex, and because it has been a first step not just toward the moving, but toward the obliteration of certain businesses and social practices, it has functioned as a massive and destructive intervention in the social fabric of a noncriminal group in the city—an intervention I for one deeply resent.

If the range of heterosexist homophobic society as a system wants to ally itself to an architecture, a lifestyle, and a range of social practices that eschew contact out of an ever inflating fear of the alliance between pleasure and chaos, then I think it is in for a sad time, far more restrictive, unpleasant, and impoverishing than the strictures of monogamy could ever be.

The thousands on thousands of gay men, contingently "responsible" or "irresponsible," who utilized the old Times Square and like facilities for sex already know that contact is necessary. I would hope this essay makes clear that it is necessary for the whole of a flexible, democratic society—and I feel it is only socially responsible to say so.

houses (both types), brunches, entertainment, cruising areas, truck stop sex, circuit parties, and many more—have grown up outside the knowledge of much of the straight world. But these institutions have nevertheless grown up very much *within* our society, not outside it. They have been restrained on every side. That is how they have attained their current form. They do not propagate insanely in some extrasocial and unconstrained "outside/ beyond," apart from any concept of social responsibility—and that includes what goes on in the orgy rooms at the baths. The freedom to "be" "gay" without the freedom to choose to partake of these institutions is just as meaningless as the freedom to "be" "Jewish" when, say, any given Jewish ritual, text, or cultural practice is outlawed; it is as meaningless as the "freedom" to "be" "black" in a world where black music, literature, culture, language, foods, and churches and all the social practices that have been generated through the process of black historical exclusion were suddenly suppressed. I say this not because a sexual preference is in any necessary way identical to a race, or for that matter identical to a religion. (Nor am I proposing the equally absurd notion that a race and a religion are equivalent.) I say it rather because none of the three—race, religion, or sexual preference—represents some absolute essentialist state; I say it because all three are complex social constructs, and thus do not come into being without their attendant constructed institutions.

Tolerance—not assimilation—is the democratic litmus test for social equality.

• • •

§10.4. It is impossible to hear such urban proposals as these and not think imme-diately of gender differences, divisions, barriers . . .

Our marginal consideration of "feminized" and "masculinized" poverty at §I has already suggested what here I must articulate. That so many women suffer "feminized poverty," that so many men suffer "masculinized poverty," as well as that more and more of the "wrong" sex show up in each, are not demonstrations of psychological difference but are rather an all but crushing demonstration that, in the Symbolic space of the class war, men and women are primarily different so-cioeconomic classes, formed by different political and socioeconomic forces. In-deed, they demonstrate just how powerful these class markers are, since, in a soci-ety where men and women relate as they do and regularly cohabit and marry, such markers cut through that all-important public/private boundary, even when it is comfortably in place.

"Traditional psychological differences" between genders, when they occur, are replicating superstructural elements that work to stabilize a basic infrastructural situation; and the basic structure that grounds patriarchal (i.e., heterosexist) soci-ety is one of artificial sexual scarcity—that is to say, an institution to fulfill the un-stated mandate of the state to produce a certain number of children who will grow up into a certain range of various socially responsible adults, performing one or more of a range of functions: parents, workers, administrators, soldiers . . .

Because of the current world population problem and changes in technology, that mandate has changed radically since the Revolution of 1848 (i.e., the last 150 years). At this point, in an age of easy birth control, it is fairly clear that the nations most likely to prevail are the ones most successful in dissociating sex from procre-ation, though this all but reverses the earliest form of the patriarchal mandate: "Go forth and multiply."

From this point, let us turn to one of the more unpleasant urban phenom-ena: the wolf whistle, the catcall, the lewd jeers and comments constantly passed

195

from men in groups and singly to women on the street—the behavior that, at his shoeshine stand at Forty-second Street and Eighth Avenue, for twenty-five years, Ben has taunted, exploited, destabilized, and aestheticised. Away from the urban center of desire Ben holds sway at, in the surrounding city streets, such comments pass as more or less ritualized expressions of hostility and aggression toward women by men who, to the extent they are thinking at all, glibly blame women for the situation of heterosexual scarcity. As every woman knows, the message that underlies such jeers and comments, no matter how much they seem to highlight her attractiveness, is not "I want to fuck *you*," but rather "I *know* you won't fuck me, no matter *how* available I make myself—so the hell with you!" The fact that at twelve-thirty in the afternoon the average construction worker on his lunch hour is no more available for a quick fuck than the average secretary on hers is not really to the question: that's what keeps it ritualized—what allows it to leap back and forth across some fibrillating boundary between the just bearable and the wholly intolerable.

Gay urban society early on learned how to overcome the sexual scarcity problem, in a population field where, if anything, scarcity could easily be even greater. Suppose heterosexual society took a lesson from gay society and addressed the problem not through antisex superstructural modifications but through pro-sex infrastructural change.

Consider a public sex institution, not like the Show World Center that Ben so decries, set up and organized for men, but rather a large number of hostels in many neighborhoods throughout the urban area, privately owned and competing to provide the best services, all of which catered to women, renting not by the day but by the hour, where women could bring their sexual partners for a brief one- , two- , three- , four-hour tryst. Such hostels would be equipped with a good security system, surveillance, alarms, and bouncers (as well as birth control material) available for emergency problems. Moreover, the management would make clear that, within its precincts, all decisions were women's call, with everything designed for women's comfort and convenience.

Some people will recognize that in many cities prostitutes (and gay men) have had access to institutions now closer to, now further from, just this model for hundreds of years. In a sense, the only change I am suggesting is to move such institutions from the barely known and secret, from the discourse of the illicit, into the widely known, well-publicized, and generally advertised rhetoric of bourgeois elegance and convenience, promoting them as a sexual service for all women, single, married, straight, gay, prostitute, or society matron.

Such a social change might actually put a dent in the system of artificial heterosexual scarcity. With the wide establishment and use of such hostels, I can't guarantee that all wolf whistles or catcalls—other than Ben's historic and histrionic parody—will fall away from our streets; but I *can* guarantee that their meaning and their hostile tenor (that is their content and form) will change radically, precisely as it becomes common knowledge among straight males that, in *this* town, you now have a statistically *much* greater chance of getting laid with a newly met woman (because, even if she doesn't want to bond her life to yours forever but just thinks you have a cute butt, a nice smile, and something about you reminds her of Will Smith or Al Borland or John Goodman, she has somewhere to take you), and that the best way to exploit this situation of greater sexual availability is probably *not* to antagonize random women on the street.

From the population problem to the lewd street comment, there are many reasons to promote public heterosexual sex on the model public gay sex has followed for years and, in one form or another, likely will continue to follow. But *if* we are going to do such a thing, it is only sensible to put its control into the hands of women and set it up for their use and convenience from the start.

My active proposals do not extend to such utopian small-business sexual assignation hostels for women. Still, nothing in my argument precludes them.

What we must recall from our current theory, from our historical practice, is that such institutions and the resultant social contact practices they would develop and contour would no more overturn and rot our society than has alcohol, pop music, the novel, the opera, tobacco, the nightclub, any number of recreational drugs, makeup, men's clubs, tea-room sex among gay men, universal white male suffrage, lending libraries, comic books, black suffrage, women's suffrage, Catholicism, legal abortions, Protestantism, public education, Judaism, television, the waltz, coeducation, racial integration, jazz, the pin-up, the pornographic film, body piercing, bundling, taffypulls, tattoos, the fox trot, films, the theater, laws repealing the death penalty, beauty parlors, the university, laws preventing child labor, church marriages for the working classes—or any other social institution that is now, or was once, decried from one podium, pulpit, or another as the End of Civilization as We Know It. Such institutions are always already within the social; indeed they *are* the social—and are not outside it. That is why they all require social intelligence in their administration. All are always already in tension with other institutions. That is why they all have at one time or another required more or less vigilant protection as a set of freedoms.

§10.5. Interclass contact conducted in a mode of good will is the locus of democracy as visible social drama, a drama that must be supported and sustained by political, educational, medical, job, and cultural equality of opportunity if democracy is to mean to most people any more than an annual or quatra-annual visit to a voting booth; if democracy is to animate both infrastructure and superstructure. The supports and guys that stabilize such contact must be judicially enforced and legally redressable. It is not too much to say, then, that contact—interclass contact—is the lymphatic system of a democratic metropolis, whether it comes with the web of gay sexual services, whether it comes through the lanes of heterosexual services (and such gay and straight services include but are in *no* way limited to heterosexual and homosexual prostitution!), or in any number of other forms (standing in line at a movie, waiting for the public library to open, sitting at a bar, waiting in line at the counter of the grocery store or the welfare office, waiting to be called for a *voir dire* while on jury duty, coming down to sit on the stoop on a warm day, perhaps to wait for the mail—or cruising for sex), while in general they tend to involve some form of "loitering" (or, at least, lingering), are unspecifiable in any systematic way. (Their asystematicity is part of their nature.) A discourse that promotes, values, and facilitates such contact is vital to the material politics as well as to the vision of a democratic city. Contact fights the networking notion that the only "safe" friends we can ever have must be met through school, work, or preselected special interest groups: from gyms and health clubs to reading groups and volunteer work. Contact and its human rewards are fundamental to cosmopolitan culture, to its art and its literature, to its politics and its economics; to its quality of life. Relationships are always relationships of exchange—semiotic exchange at the base, in a field where, as Foucault explained, knowledge, power, and desire all function together and in opposition within the field of discourse. To repeat: Contact relationships cannot be replaced by network-style relationships because, in any given network group, the social competition is so great that the price on social materials and energies exchanged is too high to effect emotional, if not material, profit. If we can talk of social capital (for those who enjoy a truly outrageous metaphor): While networking may produce the small, steady income, contact both maintains the social field of "the pleasant" and provides as well the high-interest returns that make cosmopolitan life wonder-filled and rich.

Works Cited

Althusser, Louis. "Ideology and Ideological State Apparatuses." In *Lenin and Philosophy*. New York: Monthly Review Press, 1971.

Benderson, Bruce. *User*. New York: Dutton, 1994.

Berman, Marshal. "Signs of the Times: The Lure of Times Square." *Dissent*, Fall 1997.

Bradbury, Ray. *The Martian Chronicles*. New York: Doubleday, 1951.

Dangerous Bedfellows (Ephen Glenn Colter, Wayne Hoffman, Eva Pendleton, Alison Redick, David Serlin), eds. *Policing Public Sex: Queer Politics and the Future of AIDS Activism*. Boston: South End Press, 1996.

Flaubert, Gustave. *Sentimental Education*. Trans. Robert Baldick. Reading: Penguin Classics, 1964.

Foucault, Michel. *Michel Foucault: Ethics, Subjectivity and Truth*. Vol. 1 (*Dits et écrits*). Ed. Paul Rabinow. New York: New Press, 1994.

———. *The Order of Things: An Archaeology of the Human Science*. New York: Pantheon, 1971.

Freud, Sigmund. *Leonardo da Vinci and a Memory of His Childhood*. Trans. Alan Tyson. New York: Norton, 1964.

Gilfoye, Timothy J. "From Sourbrette Row to Show World: The Contested Sexualities of Times Square between 1889 and 1995." In *Policing Public Sex*, ed. Dangerous Bedfellows.

Gordon, Richard. "The Computerization of Daily Life, the Sexual Division of Labor, and the Homework Economy." Silicon Valley Workshop conference, University of California at Santa Cruz (1983), cited in Haraway.

Haraway, Donna. "A Cyborg Manifesto." In *Simians, Cyborgs, and Women*. New York: Routledge, 1992.

Jacobs, Jane. *The Death and Life of Great American Cities*. New York: Vintage Books, 1961.

Marcus, Steven. *The Other Victorians*. 2d ed. New York: Norton, 1974.

Pater, Walter. *The Renaissance: Studies in Art and Poetry*. 1893 text, edited, with textual notes, by Donald L. Hill. Berkeley: University of California Press, 1980.

Rechy, John. *City of Night*. New York: Triangle Classics Edition of the Quality Paperback Bookclub, 1994.

Rilke, Rainer Maria. *The Notebooks of Malte Laurids Brigge*. Trans. Stephen Mitchel. New York: Vintage Books, 1985.

Rogers, Paul T. *Saul's Book*. Wainscott, NY: Pushcart Press, 1983.

Sontag, Susan. "Notes on Camp." In *Against Interpretation*. New York: A Delta Book, 1966.

Swinburne, Algernon Charles. "An Interlude." In *The Poetry of Swinburne*, with an introduction by Ernest Rhys. New York: Modern Library, n. d.

Vaid, Urvashi. *Virtual Equality*. New York: Anchor Books, 1995.

About the Author

Born and raised in Harlem, Samuel R. Delany is a renowned novelist and critic. In addition to receiving the William Whitehead Memorial Award and the Kessler Award for his lifetime contribution to lesbian and gay writing, Delany was recognized by the *Lambda Book Report* in 1988 as one of the fifty people to most influence our conception of queerness over the past hundred years. Delany was also the subject of the documentary film *The Polymath* by award-winning filmmaker Fred Barney Taylor, which debuted in 2007 at the Tribeca Film Festival.

The paired essays that compose this book were written toward the end of Samuel R. Delany's eleven years as a professor in the Comparative Literature department at the University of Massachusetts Amherst, during which he lived on New York City's Upper West Side. Over the next two years, Delany taught English at SUNY Albany and SUNY Buffalo. Then, for fifteen years, he was professor of English and Creative Writing at Temple University, where, besides teaching both graduate- and undergraduate-level creative writing, he taught courses on Freud, lyric poetry, male sexuality, literary theory, the long novel, the graphic novel, the African American novel, and science fiction.

For three of those years, Delany was Director of Temple's Graduate Creative Writing Program, a job at which, in his own words, he was "abysmally incompetent," before he stepped down when he discovered it required knowing computer systems he hadn't even realized existed. In 2010, he was a judge on the board of fiction for the National Book Awards.

Delany's eight other essay collections (and two collections of letters, and two more of journals) present him as one of our great academic generalists. His novels include *Dhalgren* (1975), the Stonewall Book Award–winning *Dark Reflections*

(2007), *Through the Valley of the Nest of Spiders* (2012), and *The Mad Man* (1994). His 1968 novel *Nova* will reappear in a Library of America anthology, *American Science Fiction: Four Classic Novels 1968–1969*, in 2019.

Today, Samuel Delany lives with his partner of twenty-eight years, Dennis Rickett, in Philadelphia.

More information about his books and his life can be found on his website, samueldelany.com.

Robert F. Reid-Pharr is Professor of Studies of Women, Gender, and Sexuality at Harvard University. He is the author of four books: *Archives of Flesh: African America, Spain, and Post-Humanist Critique* (NYU Press, 2016), *Once You Go Black: Choice, Desire, and the Black American Intellectual* (NYU Press, 2007), *Black Gay Man: Essays* (NYU Press, 2001), and *Conjugal Union: The Body, the House, and the Black American* (1999).